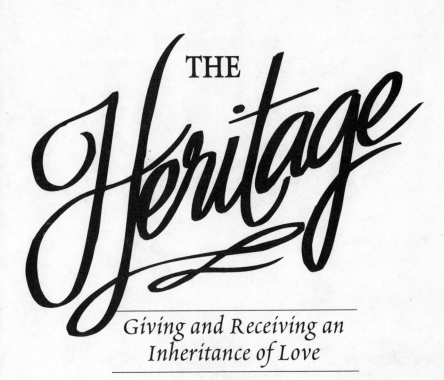

THE

Heritage

Giving and Receiving an
Inheritance of Love

KURT D. BRUNER &
J. OTIS LEDBETTER

MOODY PRESS
CHICAGO

ISBN: 0-8024-5565-4

1 3 5 7 9 10 8 6 4 2

Printed in the United States of America

To Gail Ledbetter,
who has passed on a wonderful heritage
and models what it means to give
an inheritance of love

And to Olivia Bruner,
who inspires the hope of new beginnings
by giving even though she did not receive

CONTENTS

PREFACE

As coauthors of this book, our relationship is much more than professional. Kurt and I have been like family for the past twelve years. But beyond a deep friendship, we share a passionate belief in the value of giving and receiving an inheritance of love. That's the main reason we have written *The Heritage*.

The insights and advice we will offer come from two distinct perspectives. Kurt has young children and is still in the process of building a heritage for his family. He shares as a fellow learner, drawing more from his professional experience than personal experience. Otis, on the other hand, has spent the past two decades in pastoral ministry within the local church, teaching and counseling families through the heritage-passing process. He has successfully raised two grown children, both of whom have married and started the heritage process in their own homes. Otis and Gail have one teenage daughter still in the nest.

Kurt has been helping families the past eleven years through his ministry with Focus on the Family, including seven years overseeing the Correspondence and Research department. There his colleagues handle thousands of letters and calls every week from those seeking advice as they try to build a solid heritage in the home (and from those trying to overcome the fallout of their own weak heritage). Meanwhile Otis and his wife, Gail, continue to lead seminars nationally on how to pass along a lasting heritage.

The Heritage describes in Part 1 how you can pass along a loving heritage that cares for the spiritual, emotional, and social needs of your children. In Part 2, the "Heritage Tool Chest" provides four tools for establishing a heritage in your family. In Part 3, we look at several issues that influence your ability to pass along a healthy heritage, including how to deal with a poor heritage. Even if your parents gave you little or no godly heritage, you can create a significant heritage that gives your children joy and purpose and honors your name and your God.

The first-person voice used throughout belongs to Otis, who offers many of the personal anecdotes from his ministry as a pastor and counselor. Both Kurt and I will invite you into our lives as we tell stories about our wives and children, and about the good and poor choices we made as we have tried to create a godly heritage for our families.

Join us as we share our passion for The Heritage.

ACKNOWLEDGMENTS

I f anyone could write a book alone, God could. But He used over forty men to pen His timeless masterpiece. Even today, He depends upon others to complete His eternal Book of Life. Obviously, the creation of this book required the assistance and encouragement of many others. We'd like to express our appreciation to several of them.

To those whose silhouettes are chronicled in this book —we say thanks for allowing us to share your stories.

To Al Janssen, who pointed us in the right direction by helping us focus our creativity, and Jim Vincent, our editor, who helped to fine tune our work.

I (Otis) am grateful to my good friend and secretary, Sherry Krigbaum. How could I ever complete even a day's work without your picking up the slack and organizing my schedule? Thanks for endless hours typing and editing the manuscript.

I also wish to thank Les and Sheryl Engstrom, my Aquilla and Priscilla in the ministry. Thanks also to Kathy Laughlin for her straightforward editing.

Lloyd and Mimi Ledbetter set the compass and are responsible for giving me the strong heritage that has guided me to set my life's sail properly; and Louis (Jack) and Margaret Hover have taught Gail what a heritage can and should be. I am grateful for the support and example of those two sets of parents.

Introduction
WE ALL WEAR HAND-ME-DOWNS

C onnections. Whether it's an elderly gentleman listening to the opinionated talk radio host or a stamp collector on the Internet asking about a rare stamp, we try to stay connected with the people in our lives. Connections are why a minister announces an engagement of a young couple one Sunday evening, and why the congregation breaks into applause. Connections are one way we keep this big world smaller, simpler, and more intimate. And when it comes to our own families, connections are even more vital. In fact, when we are born, each of us enters this world with strong connections to preceding generations. You cannot escape the ties of biology and identity that tie you to your parents and their parents, going back for generations.

Your connections to preceding generations can bring the good or the bad. In turn, your connections to your children and their children have a direct impact upon future generations for good or bad. This book is about choosing the good over the bad.

The impact of our ancestral links often reaches across three, four, or even five generations. Those connections may dictate many of the patterns and expectations we carry through life.

Part of this process grows out of genetic inheritance. Good health or bad, physical beauty or not, chemical imbalance or stability all flow out of the biological link each of us has to those who have gone before. Our genetic makeup, handed down through a long line of ancestors, dictates part of who we are.

But our ancestral connection goes beyond physiological characteristics to link up with a spiritual dimension. This spiritual dynamic can have far-reaching implications for one generation after another. God Himself highlighted this principle when He gave Moses the Ten Commandments; He told the nation Israel, "I, the Lord your God, am a jealous God, punishing the children for the sin of the fathers to the third and fourth generation of those who hate me, but showing love to a thousand generations of those who love me and keep my commandments" (Deuteronomy 5:9–10).

God made clear that He allows the consequences of ancestral sin to impact several generations. On the flip side, He also allows the descendants of those who love and obey Him to reap the positive results of Grandpa's and Grandma's good deeds and obedience to God.

This pattern can be observed all around us. For instance, a very high percentage of abused children end up beating their own kids. Those raised by a drunk often become adult alcoholics themselves. Criminals tend to raise criminals. Dysfunction breeds dysfunction. Moral weakness fosters moral weakness. Of course, there is also a positive side. Responsible, loving parents tend to instill the same in their offspring, and they in theirs, and so on. The good is passed from generation to generation just like the bad. If we are smart, we'll find a way to make this principle work for us rather than against us.

* * * *

My wife, Gail, is on the platform speaking to a group of women. She points to the mannequin next to her, covered in a gorgeous antique wedding gown, its exquisite ecru lace shining in the light. With its ruffles of lace over the bodice, tiny, cinched-in waist, long sleeves trimmed with more lace, and long ruffled overskirt, it has caught the audience's attention, though they still hear Gail's every word.

"Some beautiful bride wore this elegant gown on her wedding day in the early part of this century. What do you think of the train?" Gail asks, gesturing to the sheer fabric, edged with a double ruffle of lace and spread behind the gown. Gail displays this lovely Victorian gown as a symbol of the wonderful heritage that was handed down through her parents from past generations. Though this wedding gown is not her own, it reminds her of the pure and lovely heritage she desires to give to our children.

In the course of her message, she speaks of a young lady she calls "a trophy of God's grace. I'll call her Mary," Gail says. "Mary was a street-wise drug user. Sometimes she lived on the streets. Her body had the marks of drug abuse—the dirty hair, darkened eyes, the sometimes-quick movements. She had become a prostitute, selling her body and sexuality for money. But at age thirty, Mary was sick of her way of life, the occasional hunger pangs, the cold, and the dirt. Through the outreach of a local church, she came to know Jesus Christ. Her life took a 180-degree turn. Now, when Mary speaks about her turning to Christ, people are awed that she survived the drugs and admire her courage to escape a situation that had deeply entangled her."

Interestingly, Mary and Gail are both trophies of grace. Mary, of course, has seen God's grace as she recovered an innocence lost. Gail continues to see God's grace as she preserves what was carefully handed to her from past generations and sends it on to our children: a heritage of love and wisdom that will strengthen the Ledbetter name and honor the God we love.

On the platform, Gail reaches for some rags that have been hidden from the audience. The shredded clothes are soiled and threadbare. She begins to contrast them with the beautiful wedding gown.

"What were you handed?" she asks. "Were you handed rags? If so, are you content to continue wearing them? Or were you handed a Victorian gown? If so, will you continue to wear it? Believe it or not, some of us reject the gown for rags. Others, like Mary, reject the rags and begin to sew an exquisite gown for our children and children's children.

"You can choose what you will wear. You may not have any control over what you were given, but you can choose what you will wear today."

It just doesn't seem fair, does it? Some were given a wonderful, healthy, positive heritage—a beautiful gown. Others were handed rags. Many of those who were given a solid heritage will find the process of passing on that tradition as natural as breathing. Others who received a very weak heritage will have no idea how to overcome the past, let alone create a positive future for the next generation. The good news is that both can create and give a wonderful heritage. Yes, the process of doing so will be much harder for some than others; but it can be done. It must be done. How? By reclaiming what you lost, or by learning to give what you didn't get.

What are you wearing? How have the patterns of past generations influenced your life today? Did your heritage include more negative than positive? Or, as a woman, have you been handed a beautiful gown, only to wear rags of your own making? As a man, have you received a royal robe but choose instead to wear a tattered coat? Even if you have received rags, you can now replace them with a lovely gown of feminine grace or royal robe of masculine dignity.

As you move through the pages of this book, we will introduce several key principles and practices that can help you to give an inheritance of love. We will help you better understand your own heritage with three self-evaluations of your heritage (in chapters 3–5), which will give you a clear picture of your past. We will be looking at some "Leading Legacy Indicators," which will let you measure what strong and weak legacies for your children look like. You also will evaluate where you are through several inventories and projects in "Getting Personal" (in Part 2). And we will examine the impact of emotional, spiritual, and relational "hand-me-downs." We all wear them. But we can choose what they will look like. Our goal is to make our heritage work for us rather than against us by discussing several steps for overcoming the bad while embracing the good.

In Part 2 we will open the heritage tool chest. There you will learn how to create a unique "family fragrance," an atmosphere of love and safety that can permeate your home and warm the hearts of all who live there. We will discuss how to create "impression points" with your children, helping you move from accidental to intentional development of their character. You will learn how to give your children a sense of what is normal, healthy living by clarifying what we call "the right angle." And you will better understand the role of family traditions in the process of building a strong sense of personal identity. Finally, in Part 3 you will walk through the steps in creating your own heritage plan.

Most of the tips we will present are not new. But because they have been proven over time as effective methods for building a strong heritage in the home, they are well worth your time. The key to success is not deep understanding or a dramatic creativity. The key is the commitment to and the discipline of continuing the process. One of our objectives is to place the tools in your hands that will make doing so as easy and effective as possible.

We have three specific goals in *The Heritage:* (1) to help you strengthen your roots by understanding and passing the good aspects of the heritage you were given; (2) to let you break the cycle of hurt by leaving the bad behind; and (3) to assist you in charting a new course as you build a positive heritage for yourself and those you love.

You can give, and in the process receive, an inheritance of love. Join us as we explore the possibilities!

Part One
UNDERSTANDING THE HERITAGE

*The family you come from isn't as important
as the family you're going to have.*

Ring Lardner

Chapter One
AN INHERITANCE OF LOVE

R ev. James (not his real name) pauses, the lump in his throat stalling the words he attempts to speak. He has officiated scores of wedding ceremonies before with no trouble. But this one is different . . . very different. This time he is both the minister and the father of the bride. Reverend James is giving away his firstborn daughter, Rebecca. Overjoyed and overwhelmed at the same time, he swallows hard and pushes ahead, carefully following his prepared notes to avoid eye contact with his precious little girl.

"Justin," he says to the groom, his chin set and a determined inflection in his words, "my wife and I have prayed for you for twenty years and four months . . . petitioning God to keep you pure. We didn't know who you were, but that nameless prayer was fervent, as I'm sure was the case with your parents for the girl you would someday marry."

A hush seems to overwhelm the sounds of birds and traffic at the outdoor ceremony, and the witnesses listen closely to the minister's words.

"For three generations it has been the wish of the parents and grandparents on both sides for a heritage to be passed to you for safekeeping, so . . ." his voice lowers as he calmly speaks the words, "we are handing you a heritage. Now it is your responsibility. You can throw it away; many do. But our hope and prayer is that you will carry it on and give your own children what we have worked so hard to pass on to you."

As he speaks of the heritage she is being handed, his daughter finds her mind racing through many strong memories of her childhood. Becky recalls the time when, as an eight-year-old, she had taken money from her mom's jewelry box and how her parents had confronted her with the theft. That one event remains a vivid reminder of the value of trust. Her parents used the jewelry box to teach her how priceless a commodity trust is to their family.

And in a flash she remembers all the Christmas and Thanksgiving holidays and even some of the ordinary evening meals of every weekday—where Mom prepared a special time free of all distractions, and where Becky learned so many of the values she now claims as her own.

Funny . . . she thinks, as she remembers how Dad cleared his schedule for ten months and every Tuesday through Saturday drove her to and from cosmetology school. Besides their conversations in the car, there were those silly "head-banging" shenanigans during the thirty-minute drives to school. *Funny, here's Dad all dressed up and formal, and there we were, the windows rolled down at a crowded intersection and Dad and I singing away to the startled pedestrians. And once we pretended to be a crabby old couple, mad at everyone else on the road. Ha!* She remembers: Dad and she had laughed themselves to tears at people's reactions. *And then there was the time . . .*

Becky's attention snaps back to the present as her grandfather approaches the wedding kneeling bench. The heritage of her father is in her, though she is not fully aware of it.

As Grandpa turns toward Justin and her, Becky watches as his right hand plays with something in his pocket. *I wonder what he has. Or maybe he's just nervous. No, not Grandpa . . .* Her grandfather looks at them both and speaks.

"Justin and Becky, your grandma and I have prayed for this moment. The heritage we handed to your mother and father, they now give to you." His hand comes out from his coat pocket. He reveals four dimes and places them before the couple on the altar. "Here are two dimes for each of you. When troubles come, and they always do, use these dimes as a reminder to call, day or night . . . they are a part of the heritage you received from us. We will always be there for you, Becky. And we will always be there for you, Justin."

Now Justin's father approaches the couple. Chuck is choked up, on the verge of tears. He has spent the last twenty years trying to show his son how much he loves him . . . and now, it is time to say good-bye.

For years he took Justin to a little hole-in-the-wall restaurant every couple of months, where the two would talk over breakfast. It was during such times that he tried to communicate what life may hold for his boy. It was there that Chuck held his own classroom on values and ethics. It was there he allowed his son the freedom to question— to question motives and attitudes—and to get what his dad called "some country smarts" about family living.

It was just a few months before this ceremony that Chuck fronted Justin the money to strike out on his own business venture. He trusts Justin. He trusts that the heritage passed to his son from the generations before will be in hands that will keep it safe.

The hope in his heart and the anticipation is just too much. Chuck opens his mouth and utters his son's name, but then the emotion overwhelms him. The crowd waits for him to finish his prepared comments. Chuck's tears speak louder than words . . . Justin is very loved.

In the midst of this touching scene, Sarah[1] watches from the very last row and feels the resentment building. *Well, they may care for their kids and they can thank God all they want, but I think God is unfair. He picks and chooses who will have happiness in life. And I'm not one of the chosen.*

A smirk appears on Sarah's face. Though she came from a solid home much like the bride and groom did, Sarah considers this "heritage bunk" *a joke . . . "pie in the sky." It's certainly not a blessing.*

Sarah has shoved the memory of her days growing up as a teenager into the dark crevices of her mind. She wants to forget her heritage, especially the times she scoffed at her family for being so devout. That heritage, Sarah concluded, would make her miss what this life has to offer. *Hey, I'm not going to allow life to pass by without grabbing at least a couple of handfuls of happiness,* she has told herself more than once.

Watching the ceremony, she is unaware of the rebellion of her past, and somehow she is able to transfer blame onto the shoulders of her parents . . . and to the God she feels passed over her. She is single, dissatisfied with her job, and angry with her parents. And there is a skeleton in her past that she cannot tell her parents about.

The smirk on her face is only a Sunday yawn compared to the hidden anger about her past. She feels abandoned . . . isolated. Yet, the irony of it all is that in the deep part of her soul, she longs for it to work for her. But the effort to carry on the heritage is too strangling to the belief system and lifestyle she finds herself buying into. So . . . she paints on the small smile to hide the tears.

As Sarah and the other witnesses observe the ceremony wind to a conclusion, only a few realize that the event symbolizes more than a union of two lives. A heritage is being passed to a next generation, and the wedding is a significant handoff during a generations-long marathon relay. The couple's parents have spent better than twenty years fighting for and guarding the treasure they were being handed. The days and months and years of training are being celebrated at the wedding. Yet even if no guests had shown, the handoff would still have taken place; the ceremony still would have been meaningful. The grandparents would still have given their blessing to Justin and Becky as a couple worthy to handle and keep this heritage.

The minister performs his legal obligation. Reverend James prays a blessing upon the couple and then declares Justin and his daughter "husband and wife." The happy couple bounces away with their entourage following arm in arm.

During the next two hours, the moderating temperature cools the wedding crowd who gathered for this magnificent Friday evening. The cake and punch are almost gone, the sun bids farewell, and the "tiki" torches and twinkle lights begin to accept their role of lighting the romantic setting for the evening.

The three hundred chairs are empty except for one lone figure. Jim has found a seat smack in the middle of the sea of white chairs. He stares straight ahead across the small lake to the lighted, empty gazebo, where the string quartet has entertained the crowd. He isn't a loner, he isn't pouting, he isn't even just resting a weary body. He is contemplating what he has just witnessed. Yet if anybody has a reason to mock what has just taken place, it is Jim.

His father had chucked it all, messing up his own life and his family's as well. After he "fell in love" with his wife's best friend, he left the family and soon became involved in the drug culture. Though alone, Jim's mother tried to make a go of it—tried to give her kids some semblance of a normal life. She wasn't successful.

As a young adult, Jim was a handsome young man who got plenty of invitations to make wrong choices, to escape into the world of sensual pleasures. But he was determined not to. He didn't want to be like Dad. Though his dad had given Jim a poor example of manhood in action, Jim studied diligently at the local college, resisting the school's party environment. Though his background gave him every excuse to make the wrong choices in life, Jim intended to make the right ones.

Now seated in that chair, Jim is determining . . . resolving in his own heart that he will begin: *Jill and I need to create a heritage. Yeah, we're going to begin to build a heritage to pass on to the child Jill is carrying.* He sits there alone for a long time, and when the resolve is registered and confirmed in his heart, he slaps his hands onto the arms of the chair and jerks to his feet as if standing at attention. He stands there a few seconds, lets out a big sigh, then joins the end of the reception line.

Exhausted from the weeks of preparation, the father and mother of the bride begin collecting their belongings. They are numb and ready to leave the intense high this event has pushed them to. Several friends wish them well with some clichéd comments. But a few, moved by the depth of the ceremony, give their sincere thanks.

"We saw tonight an illustration of a gut-level understanding of what we know we should do with our children," says one church member. Pastor James finds the comment particularly moving because it comes from a father who leads a blended family. The pastor knows that Paul is struggling yet remains committed to create a loving environment for the children that Joann and he brought into the marriage. That fragile atmosphere was strengthened tonight by virtue of what the family members had been exposed to; namely a family where three generations of commitment to a heritage brought joy and purpose to a newly wedded couple.

Among the cheering and friendly "catcalls" of their friends, the happy couple races to their car under a barrage of flying rice. As they leave for their honeymoon, Stephen sends a silent good-bye to his daughter and son-in-law and turns to help in the cleanup. He picks up trash and then breaks down the large outdoor sound system. Eventually his eyes meet the weary eyes of his wife, and with a wink at each other and a smile shared in silence, they realize the years of effort were worth it all.

The couple drives away, gleaming with joy. They have little money. But they have been given an inheritance of love. They are rich indeed!

Chapter Two
THE HERITAGE

The scene painted in chapter 1 is authentic, not some script of a melodramatic movie. The father of the bride is actually the coauthor, Otis Ledbetter. I genuinely lived the emotions of that ceremony. For months before the bride was given to the groom I repeatedly found myself with misty eyes, even in the middle of the day with absolutely no provocation. A blubbering idiot might be a good description. The questions came.

"Why are you so emotional? Is it because she's leaving home?"

"No, I want her to leave home."

"Well, is it because you are losing a daughter?"

"No, we prepared her for marriage; we want her to be married."

"Well, is it because of who she is marrying?"

"No, we couldn't have chosen a more perfect mate for her."

"Then what is it?"

The emotion was overwhelming at times. Maybe it resembles the feeling deep within a mountain climber when his boot finally catches firm ground at the summit after challenging the mountain for days. Perhaps it is like the surge of emotion that rushes into a new mother when that newborn is taken from her womb and laid on her bosom. For the first time, she sees what she has labored for and bonded to for the past nine months.

More than just the joy of the wedding and the sadness of saying good-bye to an unmarried daughter, the tears were over a heritage being passed, one that Gail and I had tried with some success to give Becky, and that Justin and she would try to continue, shaping it with their own unique style and preferences.

Like most parents, Gail and I stayed up long nights with Becky when her brow was hot with fever. We carefully doted over her when she was toddling, to keep her from a falling injury. In addition, we shared our deep values in almost every conversation; we spent thousands of dollars to educate her in a place that would uphold our values. We guided her in what to read, what and whom to listen to, how to pick her friends; we taught her what family tradition was like and how valuable the love of a family is when the outside world abandons her. We did everything in our power to protect her developing emotions.

All of this was part of giving her a heritage. At the dinner table we offered ideas for cultivating friendships, so she might build healthy relationships. Hours were spent choosing a wardrobe and learning how to maintain it. I took her on "dates" before and during the time she would "go out" with young men. During our dates, I tried to teach her social graces and how to make a man feel special; I tried to emphasize the truth that she owes nothing to any young man. Her mother showed her the skills a homemaker should acquire.

My emotions flowed freely because I realized a milestone was being passed. All that Gail and I had worked for over the years was near completion. The heritage was complete on our end. Now the job of caretaker of the heritage was changing hands, moving into another generation. The baton called heritage, so carefully preserved, was being passed. The responsibility would soon belong to Becky and Justin. Our job was soon to change. Though the early signs are very promising, only time will tell whether we did enough. Gail and I found certain comfort, though, knowing that we did our best.

WHAT IS A HERITAGE?

Every family has a heritage, a legacy passed from generation to generation. In truth, though, the heritage is something few parents really understand. Too many times we are not sure what it is or the impact that it has on our own lives—and on the lives of those we love. Let's begin with a definition:

A heritage is the spiritual, emotional, and social legacy that is passed from parent to child . . . good or bad.

Every heritage has three distinct, yet interrelated parts, like a cord with three strands: spiritual, emotional, and social. In Ecclesiastes 4:12, Solomon points to a threefold cord as a strong tie, one not easily broken, nor easily separated. The three components together are much stronger than any one or two. With a heritage cord, the rope ties one to his past, gives security in the present and hope for the future. Here is something to hold on to when life is tossing us around like a dinghy during a storm. A parent hands this golden cord to his children, who then begin their own lives apart from their parents, yet linked by the strong cord of identity and direction. The heritage cord is not unlike a three-part baton passed along the generations, complete with a family history (both the positive and the negative).

ALL PART OF A PACKAGE

Although there are three aspects to a heritage, it is unwise to overemphasize one at the expense of the other two. Our emotional, social, and spiritual dimensions are part of a package; each one heavily influences the other two. Still, it is helpful to identify the unique dynamic of each. We will be exploring their impact and importance separately in the chapters which follow. Let's briefly touch upon them here in order to understand the forest before thoroughly examining the trees.

SPIRITUAL

Many homes totally neglect this vital element of the threefold cord. For whatever reason, parents do not offer their children a spiritual basis for life. But we are all spiritual beings who need spiritual understanding and expression. Show us a person who had no spiritual training as a child, and we'll show you a person who was handed a weak heritage. Show us a person who has rejected the religious heritage he was given, and we'll show you a person with identity problems.

Our yearning for spiritual sustenance and spiritual purpose is a universally felt need, even if spiritual expression has been largely overwhelmed by the loud but hollow sounds of a godless worldview. C. S. Lewis, an Oxford scholar and agnostic who found purpose in a relationship with God, wrote about this need in his classic, *Mere Christianity*:

> If I find in myself a desire which no experience in this world can satisfy, the most probable explanation is that I was made for another world. . . . Probably earthly pleasures were never made to satisfy it, but only to arouse it, to suggest the real thing. If that is so, I must take care, on the one hand, never to despise, or be unthankful for, these blessings, and on the other, never to mistake them for something else of which they are only a kind of copy, or echo, or mirage. I must keep alive in myself the desire for my true country, which I shall not find till after death; I must never let it get snowed under or turned aside; I must make it the main object of life to press on to that other country and to help others do the same.[1]

Kurt and I embrace a Christian worldview; we both are trained in Christian theology and involved in Christian ministry. Yet, though we strongly advocate our own religious framework as the proper platform upon which to build a spiritual heritage, the principle of passing a spiritual legacy can be found in virtually all religious traditions. The French mathematician, inventor, and philosopher Pascal has truthfully observed that there is a God-shaped vacuum inside each of our souls, and only an authentic relationship with the true Jehovah God can fill the emptiness inside. We agree.

EMOTIONAL

For better or for worse, the emotional culture in which we are raised has a profound impact upon our emotional well-being as adults. Those reared in an atmosphere of love and acceptance tend to be more secure than those from a critical, distant family. If you came from a home in which affection was rarely demonstrated, you may find expressing your love more difficult than those from a family of huggers. In short, each of us is an emotional reflection of the environment in which we were raised.

In *When Anger Hits Home*, Gary Oliver and Norman Wright explain how parents influenced a child's emotional legacy:

> One of the most important factors is our home environment. Some of us grew up in homes [where] emotions were not modeled or discussed. The few emotions that were expressed were kept behind closed doors. . . .
> Others grew up in homes where emotional expression was punished and emotional repression was reinforced. Children raised in this environment either consciously or unconsciously told themselves that it wasn't safe to feel. . . .
> [With anger,] . . . some adults had a parent who was a silent sulker. Others had a parent who played the martyr. Yet others had parents who were screamers or raging hulks. . . . No matter what the style, how you saw your parents handling their anger influenced how you handle your anger now. Your past shapes your present handling of emotions.

And while the negative can be overcome, it must first be recognized. In chapter 4, we will examine the impact of whatever emotional legacy we may have been given and the importance of surrounding our own children with love and security.

SOCIAL

How we relate to others as adults often grows out of how social issues were handled in the home. It is from our parents that we learn how to treat (or how not to treat) a husband or a wife. It is with siblings that we practice the skills of sharing, caring, and, sometimes, fighting. It is with our family that we spend our formative years eating meals together, playing games together, taking vacations together, and talking together.

Hopefully, we learn something about all levels of human relationships in the process, through both laughter and pain. Those early experiences, good and bad, have left their mark on who we are and how we interact with others.

FOR GOOD OR BAD

How important is a strong family heritage? The true stories of two different families[3] dramatically illustrate the impact for good or bad of a family heritage.

The first family is the Edwardses, probably most notable for producing the famous eighteenth-century preacher Jonathan Edwards. Jonathan's father was a minister, and his mother the daughter of a clergyman. Among their descendants into the late twentieth century were fourteen college presidents, more than one hundred college professors, more than one hundred lawyers, thirty judges, and sixty physicians. The family also has given us more than one hundred clergymen, missionaries, and theology professors, and about sixty authors.

Look at the above list and you'll discover almost every great American industry has benefited from the impact of this family's contributions.

Contrast the rich heritage and impact of the Edwards' line to the influence of the Jukes family. It has been estimated that this family has cost the state of New York millions of dollars over the years. Since the eighteenth century, the Jukes have produced three hundred professional paupers, sixty thieves, and one hundred thirty convicted criminals. Fifty-five descendants were victims of sexual obsession, and only twenty ever learned a trade (and ten of these learned it in a state prison). Sadly, this family produced at least seven murderers. Is there any question that prior generations can have a direct influence over our own life patterns?

HOPE FOR THE FUTURE

And now let's consider our own heritage, today. Some of us, like Rebecca and Justin, have been given a strong, healthy heritage. We received a solid baton, placed directly into our hands. Many more, however, have received a weakened, tarnished baton. Our parents failed to protect a heritage for us, and they dropped the baton during the relay by not preparing us properly. Some of us have suffered from indifference and neglect, others from abuse, whether physical, sexual, or constant verbal assault. Many of us will identify with Jim in chapter 1, reared in a one-parent home after his father walked out. Yet his outcome reminds us that one poor baton pass doesn't mean the heritage cannot continue. Though he didn't receive a good heritage, he is determined to give one nonetheless. His resolve is the first step toward restoring the tarnished baton he received. The same can be true for you as well.

Understanding the impact of your heritage is vital to the process of living. It can give you a new perspective on your past, a calm confidence in the present, and a meaningful sense of vision for your future. And it all starts with an understanding of the whats, whys, and hows of giving and receiving a heritage. Whether you received a wonderful heritage and are determined to pass it along to your own children or you grew up in a home filled with anger, disharmony, or abuse, we will offer some practical tools for creating a heritage for your children, embracing the good of your past while replacing the bad, and filling the void in your soul with a healthy sense of identity.

BREAKING THE CYCLE

In truth, none of us were handed a perfect heritage. We have received a mix of good and bad, because our parents, learning by doing and limited by their own weaknesses, did not always offer what was needed. My children, for example, had what some would consider a fortunate break being raised in a minister's home. But they will tell you today that "life in the fishbowl" was anything but a picnic. They were constantly held to a different standard by those around them, and their mother and I often expected more than we should have. They, like all of us, received both good and bad. Even with her positive heritage, Becky had to endure a few insensitive moments and misinformed judgments from me.

Receiving a mix of the good and the bad means your heritage may include a very good emotional legacy, while the spiritual and social elements of your heritage are weak. Or you may have received a positive spiritual legacy, but your emotional and relational heritage leave much to be desired. The risk is that we will focus so heavily upon the negative that we overlook the positive. We are too quick to reject the entire inheritance we were given due to the unpleasant parts.

In the process of closing off the pain, we can also close off our link to the past. That is not healthy. It undermines our sense of identity and stifles our ability to grow. Rejecting what we've been handed is not the solution. We should rather seek to understand it and build upon it. We must identify and keep the good, while sorting out and replacing the bad.

Here are four people who are trying to do just that. Dedicated to passing on the heritage, they are struggling because of a faulty baton pass from their parents. We will return to them throughout the book.

CATHY'S STORY

Cathy, twenty-nine and married, rejected the inheritance from her parents she had been given and had no desire of building and passing a heritage to her children. Now, as the children are growing, she begins to realize that they are suffering from the fallout of her own disillusioned past.

Cathy's parents had been ministers, but they found the demands of ministry life too much; they gave up on their dream of reaching the world with the good news and resigned their commission. They had spent much time with Cathy, sharing and living their values, and the foundation for a strong heritage was in place. But the disappointment and exhaustion after they left their ministry call began to drive the husband and wife apart. Within a matter of months, they began living separate lives. They rarely spoke to each other and both struggled with the uncertainties of the future.

Watching from the sidelines, Cathy's hurt was numbing. The fragile sense of identity she had been building began to fade right in front of her. The thoughts plagued her mind. *Mom and Dad don't really love each other. Maybe they never really loved me either.*

Her parents finally divorced, and her brothers and sisters scattered, carrying their own crop of bitterness with them. After having been handed a good heritage, Cathy watched her parents undermine what she had received. What at one time made perfect sense to her—what at one time made her comfortable—had now shaken her at her foundation. Cathy began questioning every spiritual, emotional, and social aspect of the heritage they wanted to give her.

As a result, the pendulum swung from one extreme to the other in all three areas. Before the collapse of her parent's marriage, she could handle practically any emotional strain. She had been a very strong, good-humored, level-headed young lady. Afterward, she would fly off at the slightest challenge to her opinion. She seemed always on the edge of an angry outburst or else on the verge of tears.

"Before the divorce, I enjoyed the warmth of a close-knit family and strong friendships," Cathy told me with regret in her voice. "Afterward, I went so far as to telephone any relative who dared to show they cared, ordering them to stay out of my life. Having alienated them all, I began entering into very unhealthy relationships." She dated abusive boyfriends and hung out with negative and irreverent girlfriends. She looked to them for acceptance, but they only served to undermine her identity even further.

As we talked further, I discovered that her spiritual life went from a vital source of joy to a haunting source of bitterness. "I began to see God as a bully, a mean-spirited ruler without a real heart. A deity, yes . . . but a deity who doesn't care much about me." Yet down deep, she wanted more. She scurried from church to church to church, trying to find the God she needed, while rejecting the God she had known.

Can Cathy recapture the heritage she lost? She sincerely wants to, fearful that her children will also settle for an incomplete heritage. Her desire is the first step in picking up the tarnished baton and passing on a worthwhile heritage.

PAUL AND JOANN: THE BLENDED FAMILY

In chapter 1 you met Paul and Joann, who are trying to create a heritage for a blended family created from previous marriages. Paul had thanked the pastor for giving them "a gut-level understanding of what we know we should do with our children." Creating harmony in a blended family is a major feat in itself. Many times I have met with this beautiful couple to help point them in the direction of a healthy heritage for their kids.

Paul is a tall, balding fellow with a broad vocabulary and a keen mind. Joann, approaching middle age, is an attractive woman and a bottom-line person. When talking to Joann, you sense the need to get to the point . . . cut to the chase . . . skip the gory details. Neither Paul nor Joann blame their ex-mates for the failed marriages. They are just determined to make this marriage strong, and they are committed to creating a heritage for their children.

But it isn't easy. They each have a daughter from their first marriages and now one daughter and one son from this union. Joann's daughter from her first marriage is now pregnant out of wedlock and has no plans to marry the father. Paul's daughter is deeply involved in the drug culture. She lives on the streets and is a constant threat to the safety of Paul's present family. Neither Paul nor Joann was handed a decent heritage, but they want desperately to begin one for their kids. They have questions . . .

"Is it possible?"

"Is it too late for us?"

"Are we wasting our time to even try?"

"How difficult will it be?"

"Does this heritage thing really work?"

They will learn that it is possible, it's rarely too late, and "this heritage thing" has lasting rewards that—bottom-line—do work.

MEET BILLY

Billy is a young man of whom most would say, "He will never make it." Let me just make a list of his experiences and let them speak for themselves:

He was born to a couple who did not want him.

His dad was a drug user and dealer.

His mother knew nothing but the streets.

From childhood, he was a drug user himself.

He used street language and manners.

He was very angry and it showed in his fists.

He was foul-mouthed.

When Billy finally married, his anger continued and was now directed toward his wife and children. He beat his wife and became a pathological liar. Though he started school intending to help the family and himself with a better job, he eventually dropped out of school. Later he tried to drop out of life with an overdose of amphetamines.

Billy has two children, both boys. He's sitting in my office, with one desire, a good desire. "I want to put this marriage back together and begin building a strong heritage for my kids." It is possible for him to do that, as it is for anyone who has suffered similar setbacks.

ROSE'S INHERITANCE

She came into the world because of the abuse of her father. One night a drunken Joe walked into the house and ordered his wife to the bedroom. "Get upstairs and do your wifely duty!" He proceeded to empty his passions while tears fell down her face. Rose was conceived at that moment.

Rose's mother, devastated by the years of Joe's abuse and neglect and now carrying a child conceived in pain, secretly asked her mother for help. She packed up the five kids and escaped from years of abuse and disrespect. The divorce was final at about the same time Rose was born. Her mom worked hard to raise six children alone. A full-time job and night school kept her away most of the time, so Rose more or less raised herself. She had no one to advise her on right and wrong, no one to hold her when she was hurting, no one to cheer her accomplishments, no one to teach her about boys, no one to model healthy family living.

The other parents on the street didn't want their children playing with Rose or her siblings because they were ill-kept and ill-mannered. And so heartache, loneliness, and rejection became Rose's inheritance.

But that was then. Rose grew up to become Olivia Rose Bruner, wife of my coauthor and friend, Kurt. Today, Olivia is building a wonderful heritage of love for her own family. She has broken the cycle of pain from her past and is launching a new era in her home. How did she make such a dramatic transition in life? By learning how to give and receive an inheritance of love. We will tell you more of her story later. Hers is a story of hope. Hers is a story of how a person can give what she did not receive.

Olivia's story demonstrates the powerful impact of the extended heritage, where other adults extend thier heritage to children outside their own family. (See chapter 13 for specifics on how to extend your heritage.) Her experience serves as a model for much of what we have learned, and will share, about building a heritage. Remember our definition of the heritage: the emotional, spiritual, and social legacy that is passed from parent to child . . . good or bad.

As you evaluate your own experience and family heritage, do you like what you see? If so, have you identified a plan of action for passing that tradition to others? If not, are you ready to rise above the cycle of hurt and begin a new tradition for yourself and your family? The rest of this book will help you through that process. Let's begin by taking a closer look at what makes a heritage good or bad.

Chapter Three

YOUR SPIRITUAL
LEGACY

Little fingers suddenly knocked my glasses sideways on my face, and the baby in my arms let out a shriek of delight. A snicker went across the audience, and I continued to pray as best I could. But I admit my focus was interrupted, and I moved the infant farther from the microphone. I was just glad the kid didn't relieve himself into the microphone like another infant had done a few months earlier.

Baby dedications, pulpits, microphones, and a crowd of people hoping for a good laugh just don't mix to create a sacred mood, but the event indeed is very hallowed. Brian and Sherry had been blessed with the gift of life. They were so flushed with the excitement of the responsibility handed to them that they wanted their baby dedicated as soon as possible. So I accommodated their wish and made room in this day's service for their six-week-old son.

"Brian," I began, "you and Sherry understand that this ceremony has nothing to do with the immediate spiritual condition of your baby. It has everything to do with your commitment, and nothing to do with your child's commitment." They nodded and I continued.

"Your promise before God and these witnesses this morning is a vow you have intentionally and purposefully made. You are saying that you will give every effort . . . that you will see to it, by the best of your ability, that your child will have every opportunity to know God as he matures into adulthood." Again the ecstatic couple affirmed the statement with a nod.

Brian and Sherry realize that they are powerless to determine the eternal future of their little boy, yet they also are unquestionably aware of their responsibility to little Tyler.

"Your responsibility will consist of creating an environment in which the spiritual life of your child can flourish as you both instruct him in the basics of the faith." As I paused, I could sense a keen silence. Deep truth absorbed has a way of stealing your breath for a second.

WHAT IS A SPIRITUAL LEGACY?

As noted in chapter 2, every heritage includes spiritual, emotional, and social components. Therefore it is critical that we clearly understand the meaning and impact of each. Once again, the three are so heavily intertwined that we hesitate to address them separately. The last thing we want to do is reinforce the notion that they can be wholly separated from one another. One heavily influences the other two, and none stands alone in the process of giving and receiving a solid heritage.

ITS SIGNIFICANCE

Yet there is value in taking a look at the unique role of each in defining who we are and how we got that way; so let's begin by inspecting the spiritual. Some parents tend to minimize or ignore this vital aspect of life. After all, the spiritual seems the least tangible of the three. You can feel emotions and see their results; you can act certain ways and observe the outcomes in your child's social behavior. But spiritual progress is often more difficult to observe and measure, and its impact less obvious. Yet it is first and foremost of the three. In fact, your child's sense of identity and purpose depends largely upon spiritual understanding and connection. We are, first and foremost, spiritual beings. No heritage is complete, or healthy, unless it has been built upon a spiritual foundation.

ITS DEFINITION

The goal of a strong spiritual legacy is to give the child a solid foundation for living with confidence in the unseen realities of the spiritual life. In terms of how we create such a legacy, here is a practical working definition of the spiritual legacy:

A spiritual legacy is the process whereby parents model and reinforce the unseen realities of the spiritual life.

In shaping the heritage for our children, this second definition is vital. It reveals several truths about what a spiritual legacy is.

Before we explore what a spiritual legacy is, notice what it is not. A spiritual legacy is not church attendance, though involvement in a local body can strengthen the cord. A spiritual legacy is not Bible reading, though scriptural principles are a vital part of spiritual perspective. A spiritual legacy is not necessarily dependent upon formal religious instruction, though the absence of such will cause a major void in one's worldview. All of these things contribute to a spiritual legacy, yet none of them defines it.

A spiritual legacy—like our emotional and social legacies—is influenced far more by the parents' actions and attitudes than by the roles and rules of institutions or by repetitious religious practices. We can see this clearly in three elements of our second definition of a spiritual legacy.

First, the word legacy means *something resulting from, and left behind by, an action, event, or person,* according to Noah Webster's *An American Dictionary of the English Lan-*

guage (1828). In other words, a legacy is more what we do than what we say. By our actions, we model the spiritual elements in our lives for our world—and our children—to see.

Second, a spiritual legacy is a process, not an event. The dedication ceremony was only a starting point in the life of that little baby. Brian and Sherry did not give him a legacy that day. They will do so through years of consistent, sacrificial, and committed effort. We do not earn the right to celebrate a legacy until we have paid the price to build one.

Third, parents model and reinforce a spiritual legacy. Spiritual realities are more caught than taught; the child observes the parents and sees the truth of the spiritual life in action. Indeed, a strong spiritual legacy is modeled, not mandated. It occurs in the routine moments of life and is transferred over dinner table conversations. A solid spiritual legacy is more about the daily grind than it is weekly worship. Our children need to observe the spiritual life as part of normal living rather than the exclusive domain of saintly grandmothers and professional theologians.

Fourth, it prepares our children to clearly recognize the unseen realities of the spiritual life. Each of us enters this world with an intuitive awareness that life is more than the external. Foundational principles govern our existence, and they are part of the spiritual life. Unfortunately, because these principles are unseen by all and uncomfortable for many, some parents neglect this vital aspect of passing a heritage to their children. We've all heard the comments:

"I'll let my children decide for themselves when they get older."

"I don't want to be a hypocrite."

"I hated all that church stuff growing up, so I'm not going to force it on my kids."

Such comments highlight a fundamental misunderstanding of spiritual realities in our culture. We have compartmentalized our spirituality and extracted it from the rest of life. That is tragic and dangerous. Unseen realities influence our daily decisions. When we fail to clarify and reinforce them for our children, we rob them of a critical element in decision making and a vital part of their heritage.

COMING HOME

Many great Christian leaders of this century can attribute their influence to a parent's example yesterday. Billy Graham, for example, was born into a home of devout Christian parents. His father, Frank Graham, was a simple, uneducated dairy farmer. But his faith in Christ was an example for others to behold. Melvin Graham, Billy's brother, said of his father, "His hands would tremble and his voice would shake a little, but people used to love to hear him pray." His mother, Morrow Graham, spent many hours teaching young Billy Bible verses as she scrubbed his back in the washtub. Fittingly, the first one she taught him was that great text of evangelism which would later become a foundation of his ministry, John 3:16: "For God so loved the world, that he gave his only begotten Son, that whosoever believeth in him should not perish, but have everlasting life" (KJV). Prayer accompanied every meal, and each evening after dinner, the family gathered in the family room for further devotions. Frank and Morrow Graham demonstrated and reinforced unseen spiritual realities at home. How could they have known the impact their example would have on Billy, or on the world.[1]

A WAYWARD SON

Godly parents will not always succeed in passing along a godly heritage. A spiritual legacy can be abandoned by offspring. As individuals, your children must choose for themselves and may ignore your example. Franklin Graham, Billy's firstborn son, spurned his father's faith as a teenager. Sent to a Christian boarding school to learn discipline, Franklin defied the rules by smoking cigarettes, even letting fellow smokers crawl out of his small room above the school's kitchen to sneak a smoke outside; then he lied about how the tobacco smell hung about him. "I got a kick about staying one step ahead of the 'law,'" he recalled. Later, he was expelled from a Christian college after taking a coed on a weekend date and getting stranded by bad weather and staying with her overnight. He drank regularly during a summer construction project in Alaska.

Yet, he admired his dad's consistent witness and concern for him, calling his father "the man I loved and wanted to please more than anyone on earth;" he also appreciated his mother's strong yet fair discipline and her sense of humor. He credits his parents' consistent example with giving him a spiritual legacy to which he returned in his mid twenties—when sitting on a hotel bed, he "smoked a cigarette, picked up my New Testament and re-read John 3."[2]

That evening Franklin "had an overpowering conviction that I needed to get my life right with God."[3] Since then he has directed a relief agency and now is the lead evangelist for his father's ministry.

A DOUBTING DAUGHTER

Similarly, Joni Eareckson ignored her parents' faith after a diving accident as a teenager left her paralyzed from the neck down. During weeks in a hospital bed, this once playful teen watched as a nurse had to take care of her every need and as bedsores she could not feel mocked her previous active lifestyle. Joni went from fear to anger with God to depression. She asked the question why and at one point wanted nothing to do with God.

Today, Joni Eareckson Tada has become a symbol of what it means to trust God through the trials of life for an entire generation of believers. What happened? She credits a spiritual legacy from her parents. Though she did ask why God "let this happen to me," the sturdy foundation of her parents' lives caused her to seek to know God, and she was open to the message of God's love, brought to her during her depression by a young minister, Steve Estes.

Joni's parents prepared her for physical tragedy by introducing her to spiritual realities. In Joni's words, "If I were to pick out a verse that best describes the way my parents raised us, it would be Deuteronomy 11:18–19— 'Fix these words of mine in your hearts and minds. . . . Teach them to your children, talking about them when you sit at home and when you walk along the road, when you lie down and when you get up.' That passage underscores the fact that every family function can and should be sacred."[4] John and Lindy Eareckson made an early impression on Joni, providing her with a much needed foundation for what would become a serious crisis of faith.

One never knows the impact a solid spiritual legacy may have in the lives of our children, or beyond. Your children may reject the legacy, either temporarily (as Franklin and Joni did) or completely. Your duty is only to present them with the truth and leave the results with God. You may think, *I don't consider myself a spiritual giant of the faith. I'm not sure I'm the best example.* That's OK. A strong spiritual legacy does not require uncommon piety. The key, once again, is the degree to which unseen spiritual realities are recognized and reinforced at home. You can have an impact for good on your children.

THE POWER OF THE UNSEEN

The spiritual component of your child's life is always there, but it can be diminished. When I first met Billy, the second-generation drug user and wife abuser described in the previous chapter, the spiritual part of his heritage seemed nonexistent. Intensely angry and given to cursing whatever upset him, Billy's greatest handicap actually was his inability to see anything from a spiritual standpoint. During our first meeting, I found myself really hurting for him. I could not imagine anyone so spiritually void. His parents had made no effort to suggest there was a loving God. As a result, his image of God was disfigured and his view of Scripture deformed; he regarded all "religious" people as "weak-kneed crutch leaners."

For Billy, the spiritual world was indeed alien territory. No wonder his life was in tremendous need of major repair. Billy could not see the foundational *unseen* realities of life, which can be observed only by having a solid spiritual legacy. Able to see only the *seen* realities of life, he limped his way through life without even realizing he was seriously handicapped.

The power of the unseen to affect our daily lives should not be underestimated. Recently I drove my Oldsmobile Achieva into a garage as the mechanic on the other side of the garage guided me onto a rack. After I vacated the vehicle, he walked over to several chrome levers in a corner and pushed down on one. At once my three-thousand-pound car rose effortlessly from the concrete; once it was suspended on a rack six feet overhead, the mechanic walked under it to inspect. What raised the car and what held it there? It was something we feel, but cannot see. Air! Compressed air had the power to lift the car. The foundational unseen reality was air!

Similarly the spiritual legacy passed on in the heritage is the foundational unseen reality of the spirit. Deep within our children is the authority and power of either a quickened spirit that will fill the "sails" of their lives, moving them in a Godward direction, or a deadened spirit that will leave their sails drooping lifelessly around the main mast. We parents cannot be the spirit for them. But we can create that spiritual environment where they are free to question and accept spiritual truths. Such an environment will free a child's spirit to grow and mature.

THE UNSEEN REALITY OF THE CONSCIENCE

The human conscience is one unseen reality most people will acknowledge but few understand. The conscience is not the utterance of God in our hearts. Rather, it's the mechanism enabling us to tune His voice in or tune it out. If I held up a portable radio when our president was giving a national speech and exclaimed that what I was holding in my hand was the president, I would be entirely wrong. What I hold in my hand only gives me the power to hear his voice. In other words, the conscience gives us an inward sensitivity to spiritual realities. Parents wanting to pass along a solid heritage recognize and shape that sensitive mechanism called conscience.

J. Oswald Sanders compares the conscience to a thermometer.[5] The thermometer has no inherent ability to produce needed heat or cold in the room. Its function is to measure existing conditions. The conscience is similar. It does not manufacture good or bad conduct. It rather drives feelings of guilt or innocence in response to our actions and attitudes. It measures existing conditions so that we can respond appropriately.

Though a thermometer cannot be adjusted, a thermostat can. If eighty-one degrees in the house is too warm on a humid July afternoon, you can set the thermostat to seventy degrees. The air conditioning will turn on, and the thermometer will soon start its descent toward seventy. According to the apostle Paul, the conscience also can be adjusted; it has several settings. The natural pattern moves the dial from weak, to defiled, then to evil, and finally to seared (1 Corinthians 8:7; 1 Timothy 4:2; Hebrews 10:22). But on the up side, it is possible to influence the thermometer toward a good level and a pure setting. But it requires intentional diligence and an intuitive understanding of how this unseen reality works.

Some strongly disagree with the principle of depravity, but experience and revelation tell us that the human race, from birth, has a bent toward wickedness. "Man's heart is deceitful and desperately wicked," Jeremiah asserted. Incurably sick is what that means, outside of divine intervention. A. W. Tozer compares this tendency to the cravings of a dry soil, writing:

> Every farmer knows the hunger of the wilderness, that hunger which no modern farm machinery, no improved agricultural methods can ever quite destroy. No matter how well prepared the soil, how well kept the fences, how carefully

painted the buildings, let the owner neglect for a while his prized and valued acres, and they will revert again to the wild and be swallowed up by the jungle or the wasteland. The bias of nature is toward the wilderness, never toward the fruitful field.[6]

The spiritual thermostat in the lives of our children should be consistently inspected and adjusted toward the biblical norm. A lack of, or indifference to, the inspection and adjustments of the spiritual thermostat will result in a cold spiritual component and a weak heritage. Dr. Albert Siegel warns of the consequences of a seared conscience and a cold spirit:

> When it comes to rearing children, every society is only twenty years away from barbarism. Twenty years is all we have to accomplish the task of civilizing the infants who are born into our midst each year. These savages know nothing of our language, our culture, our religion, our values, our customs of interpersonal relations. The infant is totally ignorant about communism, fascism, democracy, civil liberties, the rights of the minority as contrasted with the prerogatives of the majority, respect, decency, honesty, customs, conventions, and manners. *The barbarian must be tamed if civilization is to survive.*[7]

Siegel's warning may be harsh, yet one thing is certain. Many of our children are more than halfway between a healthy family and the line that these authors have exposed. We should be willing to constantly check the spiritual temperature of those accountable to us, particularly our children. We also must be willing to make the hard decisions that demand us to adjust spiritual thermostats Godward.

THE UNSEEN REALITY OF MORAL ABSOLUTES

Another unseen reality that must be reinforced is that of moral absolutes. Just as the law of gravity, an unseen force, has a very real impact if violated, there are binding moral laws established by God Himself that must be understood and heeded. Like a compass keeping us on track by constantly pointing to true north, parents must equip a child to recognize "true north" on the journey of life. Moral character can only be developed in the context of absolute truth.

In his first book, Kurt addressed the vital importance of establishing accurate life directions based upon absolute truths. Our "life map" is only good if it is consistent with reality, pointing us in the right direction as we navigate our way toward successful living.

> Few things are as frustrating as the effort to locate a new address using a less than precise map. . . . We have arrived at many social gatherings late and tense as a result of our combined mapping efforts. . . . It can be embarrassing.
>
> Just as a reliable map is essential for getting to an unfamiliar location, our understanding of the world must be accurate if we hope to attain our objectives in life. Imagine the frustration and futility of trying to find an address in Denver using a map of Dallas. Yet, we often make important life decisions based upon a faulty worldview, and the consequences can be far worse than simple embarrassment.
>
> Each of us develops his or her life map according to various factors.[8]

Kurt mentioned "the instruction and example of our parents" as providing the earliest way children begin to understand their world. Later, teachers and peer relationships influence the developing map; finally, "exposure to the universe of ideas and belief patterns solidifies our worldview."[9] Clearly, an early, strong spiritual heritage will shape our children's view of moral right and wrong. For an accurate view of the world, our children need us to offer them clear directions, based upon timeless truths.

THE UNSEEN REALITY OF GOD'S COMMUNICATION

The third unseen reality of the spiritual component is God's ability to communicate with our children. Parents typically are able to communicate with their children on the physical and emotional levels, but what about the spiritual? As parents, we have little difficulty understanding the physical and emotional needs of our children. From birth, the little tykes let us know in various ways what they want. From letting out an infant cry, to throwing a childish tantrum, to barking a thoughtless order, to making a polite request . . . we respond to their need even while molding their ability to communicate it. When they are hungry, we feed them. When they scratch a knee, we mend the wound. When they are smarting emotionally, we sense it and respond with loving support. Their habits might change; their appetite might be lost— or become voracious. They may isolate themselves. All of which are unspoken messages that they need us.

The physical and emotional needs of a child are readily apparent, evidenced through their outward behavior. Parents can respond to these needs in tangible ways, touching the child through the five senses, which serve as our gateway to the human soul.

When it comes to making the spiritual connection, however, only God has a direct gateway into the human heart. He has created us with the capacity and desire to relate to Him. He doesn't need the five senses to speak to us. He is able to bypass our senses and go directly to the spirit. But He is the only One who can.

MAKING THE SPIRITUAL CONNECTION

The job of a parent is to understand this dynamic, recognize it when it occurs, and reinforce the unseen connection of the spiritual life. We can encourage our children to pray, listen to their questions about God, and recognize that they may be ready to hear about and understand spiritual matters sooner than we think.

The priest Eli understood this truth when Samuel, a young boy sent to Eli's home to learn to follow God, heard the voice of God one night (1 Samuel 3). Twice while asleep young Samuel heard his name called; twice he went to Eli's room, thinking the priest had called him. Both times the priest explained he had not called, and the sleepy boy returned to bed. When Samuel returned a third time to Eli's bedside, saying the priest this time must have called, the priest understood. He did not rebuke the boy but realized God was speaking and the boy must listen.

"Go and lie down," he instructed the boy, "and if He calls you, say, 'Speak, Lord, for your servant is listening.'" So Samuel did. And as a result of being tuned in to His voice, Samuel met God and became the avenue through which the Lord spoke to His people.

Eli understood the unseen reality of the spiritual world and knew how to help Samuel connect with God's voice. Parents have the same responsibility when it comes to their children. We must first be sensitive to God's voice ourselves . . . know how to recognize it . . . and then create an environment which allows our children to do the same. The end result? They will know the Lord.

As Pascal has said, a "God-shaped vacuum" exists in each of us, even as children. Our children desire to fill that vacuum, and God wants to communicate through that vacuum to our very hearts. Parents sometimes accept the falsehood of a humanistic worldview that a child does not need or even want God on a normal basis, but is content with who he is. When we accept that view or do anything that hinders our passing on a spiritual heritage, we effectively weaken the heritage, and may be giving our children a legacy of spiritual darkness, aimlessly groping for the light.

The brilliant world leader Winston Churchill had great insight when he observed, "The destiny of man is not measured by material computation. When great forces are on the move in the world, we learn we are spirits—not animals."[10] As parents we must acknowledge that truth: both we and our children are more spiritual beings than we are physical. The spiritual component of the heritage is a vital part we must not neglect. Take care to model and reinforce for your children the unseen realities of the spiritual life.

EVALUATING YOUR OWN SPIRITUAL LEGACY

How strong was the spiritual legacy you received? This chapter concludes with an exercise designed to help you answer that question. First, though, let's briefly highlight some of the characteristics of a good and bad spiritual legacy.

TRAITS OF A GOOD SPIRITUAL LEGACY

Perhaps the most important characteristic of a good spiritual legacy is that it gives us *a foundation for understanding and responding to the work of God in our lives*. In contrast, a bad legacy will limit our ability to respond to this vital aspect of living.

A second characteristic is *balance*. Some people are so heavenly minded they become remote from those who need to hear spiritual truths. Others are so focused on people and goods in the material world that they lose track of what is truly important in life. A good spiritual legacy shows us a balance between these two extremes.

A third characteristic is *genuineness in our dealings*. That applies to how your parents presented the spiritual component to you. I have spoken with many individuals who grew up in homes where spiritual discussions were used as a means of manipulation in the home—supporting Mom or Dad's agenda rather than reinforcing the true nature of God. Others saw the spiritual life limited to Christmas and Easter church attendance, rather than a routine part of family living. Still others lived under the heavy weight of rules and regulations which were irrelevant when it came to real life. In all three cases, the spiritual component on the part of the parents was insincere, and the children picked up on that.

That was the major problem for Jim, the young man sitting alone amid the sea of white chairs at Rebecca's wedding. Jim was not passed a spiritual legacy from his parents. They weren't atheist or agnostic, but the big family Bible resting on the coffee table was little more than a prop, something to spur their own consciences as well as their children's every once in a while. They did not use the Bible as a source of absolutely reliable truth, and Jim and his siblings quickly recognized that.

EXAMINING OUR LEGACY

Before we can effectively develop a strategy for passing a good heritage to our children, it is critical that we examine the heritage we were given. Some of us received a very positive heritage; others did not. Most of us, however, received a mixed bag—certain parts were good, while other parts were not so good. Those elements which were positive, we should keep and pass on. Those which were not, we should replace. But in order to do so, we must identify which parts of our heritage may or may not be keepers.

The "Spiritual Legacy Evaluation" that concludes this chapter, as well as the emotional and social evaluations at the end of chapters 4 and 5, let you measure the heritage you have received in these three dimensions. Complete each one and you will better understand the strength of the legacy that you received.

THE LEADING LEGACY INDICATORS

When you complete the evaluation of your spiritual legacy, you may wonder, *What can I do to pass along an even better spiritual legacy for my children?* The answer to that question is more fully discussed in Part 2, when we open the Heritage Tool Chest. But in Part 1, we want to give you a preview of what you can do by giving you a list of good and bad elements for each of the three elements of the heritage—the spiritual, the emotional, and the social. We call the three previews Leading Legacy Indicators.

ECONOMIC AND CULTURAL INDICATORS

Our Leading Legacy Indicators share a kinship with the Leading Cultural Indicators developed by William Bennett and his associates. In the early 1990s Bennett, a former U.S. Secretary of Education, published a set of statistics to reflect the state of our national culture and called them the Index of Leading Cultural Indicators. Bennett included academic performance in the schools, illegitimate birth rates, juvenile crime statistics, and similar information.

His index is similar to the federal government's periodic report called the "Index of Leading Economic Indicators." That index highlights statistics that reflect the overall health of the U.S. economy, and investors and governmental leaders watch closely those economic indicators to gain a high level picture of how the economy has performed and what it may do in the months to come. Now people are considering Bennett's index as one notable way to measure the current state of America's social health: how we treat ourselves and one another.[11]

Neither the government's economic index nor Bennett's cultural index is comprehensive. But as leading indicators they provide us with one measurement of our condition, whether economically or culturally. In like manner we need to be able to measure the state of the heritage we are giving our children.

A PRACTICAL TOOL

The Leading Legacy Indicators may be less precise than the indexes of the federal government and William Bennett, yet they form an equally practical tool for measuring the state of the heritage you are giving your children. To help you evaluate the present strength of that heritage, this chapter and the next two include lists that offer measures of the legacy in the spiritual, emotional, and social realms. It's a solid way to identify the relative health of your heritage.

Below is the first list, which summarizes the Leading Legacy Indicators for the spiritual dimension of your legacy. The indicators highlight some of the key differences between a good and bad spiritual legacy. We should caution that the list states the extremes. Obviously, most of us experienced something in between the two. But it is helpful, nonetheless, as a tool for comparative evaluation.

A STRONG SPIRITUAL LEGACY . . .

• Acknowledges and reinforces spiritual realities.

• Views God as a personal, caring being who is to be both loved and respected. Makes spiritual activities a routine aspect of life (church attendance, prayer, Scripture reading, etc.).

• Talks about spiritual issues as a means of reinforcing spiritual commitments.

• Clarifies timeless truth, right from wrong.

• Incorporates spiritual principles into everyday living.

A WEAK SPIRITUAL LEGACY . . .

• Undermines or ignores spiritual realities.

• Represents God as an impersonal being, to be ignored or feared.

• Never or rarely participates in spiritual activities.

• Has few spiritual discussions of a constructive nature.

• Confuses absolutes and upholds relativism.

• Separates the spiritual from the "practical."

Again, this list is by no means comprehensive. It does, however, identify some of the key areas that affect your child's spiritual legacy. Where are you now among these indicators? At this point, is your spiritual legacy to your children more positive than negative?

Wherever you are, realize that, like Jim, it's never too late to give your child a stronger legacy as you leave your own behind. Complete the "Spiritual Legacy Evaluation" below, and then turn to chapter 4 to see how you can measure your emotional legacy.

Spiritual Legacy Evaluation

Answer each question by circling the number that best reflects the legacy you have received from your parents; then add your total score.

1. To what degree were spiritual principles incorporated into daily family life?
   1—Never
   2—Rarely
   3—Sometimes
   4—Frequently
   5—Almost always
   6—Consistently

2. Which word captures the tone of how you learned to view/relate to God?
   1—Absent
   2—Adversarial
   3—Fearful
   4—Casual
   5—Solemn
   6—Intimate

3. How would you summarize your family's level of participation in spiritual activities?
   1—Nonexistent
   2—Rare
   3—Occasional
   4—Regimental
   5—Active
   6—Enthusiastic

4. How were spiritual discussions applied in your home?

    1—They weren't
    2—To control
    3—To manipulate
    4—To teach
    5—To influence
    6—To reinforce

5. What was the perspective in your home with regard to moral absolutes?

    1—If it feels good, do it!
    2—There are no absolutes
    3—Let your heart guide you
    4—Dogmatic legalism
    5—Moderate conservatism
    6—Clear life boundaries

Results
Above 24 = Strong spiritual legacy
  19–24 = Healthy legacy
  14–18 = Mixed legacy—good and bad elements
  10–13 = Weak spiritual legacy
Below 10 = Damaged spiritual legacy

If you scored in the upper half of this self-analysis, you are blessed by an outstanding spiritual heritage. Those who receive such a legacy are rare indeed.

If your score ended up near the bottom, don't despair. There are many who have established and passed a wonderful heritage despite falling into this category. Most of us will probably fall somewhere in the middle. As stated earlier, more likely than not, we received a mixed bag.

Whatever your specific score, the goal is the same. We hope to better understand our own heritage so that we can keep and pass on the good, and replace the bad with something better. We will discuss how later.

Chapter Four

YOUR EMOTIONAL LEGACY

The radio tower at Detroit's Metropolitan Airport cleared Flight 255 for departure, and Captain John R. Maus, fifty-seven, taxied the jetliner onto runway 3-Center North. Maus, a veteran pilot with twenty thousand hours of flight experience, quickly received final clearance and pushed the throttle on the MD-80 aircraft. The plane, loaded with almost twenty tons of jet fuel and six thousand pounds of luggage, hurtled down the runway but did not rise at the normal point. Instead, it continued hundreds of feet further before lifting almost fifty feet. In the cockpit, a computer-generated voice repeated the words, "Stall . . . stall," indicating that the airflow over the wings was no longer sufficient to lift the plane; the jet was falling, not flying. The plane plunged to the ground.

Traveling at about 215 miles per hour, the plane knocked a jagged piece off the roof of a rental car building and then ricocheted off the embankment of an access road to Interstate 94. Flight 255 disintegrated into chunks of fiery metal, smashing three cars and killing at least three more people, the cars' drivers.

A GLIMMER OF HOPE

More than one hundred passengers died that day, and the real-life tragedies reported in the media were heart-wrenching. But millions watching television coverage found a glimmer of hope from the story of the miracle girl, Cecilia Cichan.

Rescue workers found Cecilia strapped in her seat, moaning. When they plucked her from the gnarled debris, they first assumed that four-year-old Cecilia of Tempe, Arizona, had been a passenger in a car hit by the falling plane. Said Sergeant Bruce Schneider of the Wayne County Sheriff's Department: "It's beyond comprehension how someone could survive something like this. It's a miracle. She had to be in the perfect spot."

Rescuers believe that Cecilia's mother, Paula, thirty-three, a registered nurse, may have saved her daughter's life by leaving her own plane seat and wrapping herself around Cecilia's seat to protect her child from the flames. The mother died in the crash along with Cecilia's father, Michael, and six-year-old brother David.

Cecilia suffered a concussion, a broken leg and collarbone, and third-degree burns on her arms and hands. But the hope-filled report in all the news articles contained the words: "She is expected to recover."

Don't you love those words, "expected to recover"? The scars from the burns will always be there; the horror of the flying debris, the noise of the banging metal and scraping sounds of a crashing, skidding, disintegrating plane may evidence itself in many ways, but Cecilia is "expected to recover."

Though more than one hundred died in the crash (including Kurt's best friend Don), a small child survived the crash when her mother responded by intentionally wrapping Cecilia's tiny body in the protective blanket of her own. Recognizing that she couldn't stop the tragedy from occurring, she did her best to engulf her daughter in an environment that would increase her chances for survival.

A strong emotional legacy can do much the same. It creates an environment of love and protection, increasing the odds for our children as they face the inevitable traumas of life. Tragedy will come. Painful experiences will invade our desire to protect them. Like Cecilia's mother, we can do nothing to stop the collision. But we can help our kids survive, and even thrive through it all.

WHAT IS AN EMOTIONAL LEGACY?

Family counselors routinely encounter clients with the lasting effects of painful childhood memories. People from all walks of life struggle to overcome a negative emotional legacy, which hinders their ability to cope with the inevitable struggles of life. Sadly, a solid emotional legacy seems to have become the exception rather than the norm. But it doesn't have to be that way. Whether or not you received a strong emotional legacy, you can give one.

For those who have spent their entire lives trying to escape the past, it is difficult to comprehend the strength and stability that a positive emotional legacy can have upon future generations. If thoughts of your childhood bring fear rather than fondness, imagine what it would be like for family memories to warm your heart rather than tighten your stomach. Now imagine yourself giving such feelings to your own children. It is possible. And the first step is understanding what an emotional legacy should be, and can be.

A strong emotional legacy will give a child healthy emotions that allow him or her to deal in a positive way with the struggles of life. Here's a definition of a strong emotional legacy:

A strong emotional legacy is that enduring sense of security and emotional stability, nurtured in an environment of safety and love.

Let's break this definition down into bite-size morsels.

First, an emotional legacy is nurtured by parents. You cannot build a solid emotional legacy quickly, like a shed or log cabin. It takes lots of time and consistency to develop in your child a sense of emotional wholeness.

The process can be compared to planting a tree. Some trees, as saplings, need a post to hold their small trunks against the wind. Most will need much time to deepen their roots, so that they can locate water far down when the drought eventually comes. Without protection and time, the tree is vulnerable to natural catastrophe—wind, drought, attacks by ground animals. But once time has passed, the tree is strong and stable for years to come.

The key to a tree's strength is deep, strong roots, and to grow strong, the roots of the tree must be planted in rich soil, as well as receive plenty of water and sunshine. So it is with our emotional legacy. We must create an atmosphere that surrounds a child's fragile spirit with the nourishment required for healthy growth. This gives the child security and emotional stability.

Second, an emotional legacy endures. It is not quickly forgotten; it typically lasts through the adult years. When the child turns eighteen years old, the end of his childhood experiences becomes the beginning of the emotional legacy, which will continue to influence his adult years.

As Kurt and I have observed and counseled hundreds of adults over the years, we have found that an emotional legacy, whether weak or strong, has a long-term impact. In my counseling experience, the parents' influence upon the children's emotional health has been an obstacle to be overcome rather than a blessing to be cherished. Diana, for example, still struggles with the mistrust and fear nurtured by a lying and abusive father. She works hard to keep those deep-rooted feelings from affecting her relationships today, but it is a constant battle.

Not all adults had that experience growing up. Janet, for instance, had a solid emotional legacy and today has little difficulty creating a strong emotional environment in her home. Diana and Janet demonstrate how childhood experiences leave a dramatic imprint upon us years after leaving home.

Last, a healthy emotional legacy gives security and stability cultivated in an environment of love and safety. More than any other aspect of a heritage, the environment and tone of family life directly influences the outcome of our emotional selves. An atmosphere of love nourishes our emotional stability, the capacity to cope with failure and pain. An atmosphere of safety provides fertile soil for our sense of security to grow deep, giving us the confidence to face a harsh and often cruel world—to beat the odds and keep our identity intact. If either love or safety is missing from the environment, deep roots are unlikely.

In short, a strong heritage can protect the fragile development of a child's emotional well-being, much like Cecilia's mother in the plane crash, by wrapping the child in an environment of support. In the process, the capacity for dealing with emotional trauma can flourish.

LIKE A STABILIZER BAR

Not long ago Van Noble, a general contractor in his thirties and a member of my church, invited me to go to an event in which he had begun to participate. As a stock car racer, Van loved the thrill and challenge of going fast and staying safe. Most fans, I found, love the loud engines, screeching tires, speed, and the chance for a couple of dramatic crashes every race. Very interesting at times, I must admit. *How in the world can a driver throw his car into a dangerous curve on the track, with the back end fishtailing and other cars hurling toward him at more than one hundred miles per hour?* I wondered. It doesn't seem very rational. If I wanted that kind of stress, why not just adopt a junior higher and raise him?

So I asked Van, "What keeps the car from crashing and burning at times like that?"

"My stabilizer bar," he answered.

Affixed somewhere on the sophisticated suspension of his car is a vital part called the stabilizer bar. Of course, it's not the only thing that creates stability, but it is important. It keeps the car from swaying excessively while leaning into a horseshoe turn. It keeps the vehicle manageable as the car roars around dangerous curves with both sets of wheels firmly on the asphalt.

The emotional element of the heritage cord is like an auto's stabilizer bar; the emotions are to act as a stabilizer to the spiritual and social components. Many a relationship has been lost because of unstable emotions, which produced irrational thinking and actions. Spiritual lives crash and burn each day while trying to navigate harsh circumstances thrown at them. Why? Because as children growing up, their emotions at some point were impaired. Now as adults, without the emotional health to give stability, the other two elements are pushed to the breaking point. As a result, either their relationships or spiritual lives (often both) are abandoned.

In chapter 1 we met Sarah, who as a teenager had rejected the heritage of her home. Sarah heaped anger and blame onto her parents, who could not figure out why she was responding so hatefully to everything they tried to do for her. What they did not know was that Sarah's anger was in reaction to an "emotional crash" she had experienced outside the home.

At age eleven, Sarah had been used as the sexual toy of a much older boy. He violated her innocence, took her virginity, and awakened emotions in her that should have been left dormant for years. Then when the boy had had enough thrills, he severed the emotional bond he had created, leaving Sarah to deal with the blunt blow on her mind and soul. She couldn't share it with her parents because she would reveal her "willing" participation.

The rest is predictable. The hurt raised its ugly head in all aspects of her life, from thoughts about God to thoughts about her parents. *God is mean! He passed me by! My parents don't care.* She even felt resentment toward her friends: They don't stay around long when things get tough.

As an adult, Sarah's emotions are still immature, back where she left them as a teen. Passing a heritage is "pie in the sky" to her.

When Sarah's life crashed as a young girl, her stabilizing bar of emotions was not strong enough to protect her. She took an emotional hit, and the impact had devastating consequences. Could her parents have helped her at the point of the trauma? Yes, her parents would have been willing to help, if they had known. Yet like many other mothers and fathers, Sarah's folks were not always able to recognize and respond to Sarah's emotions of anger and depression.

HOW TO "TAKE A HIT"

Some of us seem to absorb an "emotional hit" better than others. If you are strong emotionally, one reason is that your parents as part of the heritage gave you a strong emotional legacy. Remember, the spiritual, emotional, and relational are interdependent; the impact of an emotional hit must be distributed across the three elements of the baton. Each must support the other two.

A strong spiritual segment of the heritage helps the emotional aspect find a greater purpose for its suffering and yield a greater good. The emotional will search for a reason—a purpose to the slightest wound—in order to ease the pain it must endure. Meanwhile, when you pass on the baton with a solid social segment, your children will gladly accept the external support of other people; that can allow their emotions to "rest" in the security of love and acceptance.

Put simply, our children will better cope with the inevitable pain of life if we provide them with a strong heritage. All three elements can help them endure any hit— but the stabilizing influence of a solid emotional legacy is critical.

Our emotions—and our children's—can be damaged growing up by many things, including abuse, mistreatment or unfairness at school, even the taunting of classmates. Often the response is to give up, to trust others no more, to withdraw. As one lady, whom I'll call Sally, told me, "I have been wounded so many times that I learned to shut my emotions down." Sally actually did not shut her emotions down . . . that is virtually impossible. We are fundamentally emotional beings. What she did was begin to wrap her emotions with strands of harsh words, defensive actions, isolation, and a coolness toward anyone who might come around—friend or foe.

EMOTIONAL COCOONING

Sally was wrapping her emotions in a tight cocoon, which effectively shut everyone out who tried to move in close. Her would-be friends were kept at arm's length, and she quickly cooled any warmth they would try to show her. It was no surprise that Sally had no close friendships.

I want you to meet Ginger. Ginger is the daughter of two Christian parents who are heavily involved with their church. Brad, her father, is a forty-year-old man who is a civilian worker for the Air Force, and his wife, Anne, is a professional secretary. They both are very much in love with their two children.

As parents, we can help our children obtain an emotional legacy of security and stability. We provide an environment conducive for passing on this emotional element when we (1) ask them how things are going (and ask with real concern instead of a clichéd question), (2) listen to them as they talk about their feelings, and (3) model emotional honesty with them—showing our own angers and fears—as we try to handle our feelings in the right way.

Ginger's parents sought to help their daughter before the emotional cocoon wrapped too tightly around her. For them, outside help was vital; sometimes that will be necessary for you as well, as your child is unable, due to an actual or perceived threat, to talk directly to you. Initially her mother, Anne, delayed and denied Ginger's problem.

But Anne soon acknowledged the warning signs and cared enough to pursue the issue.

The counseling director noticed Ginger's abnormal behavior: violent outbursts and spitting at the students and at the teacher. At times, the seven-year-old girl would seem almost crazy with rage. Ginger also began to gain weight quickly. Her mother took her to a doctor and found nothing physically wrong. The behavior persisted even at the threat of a complete expulsion from the school she was attending.

Anne was stumped by her daughter's actions and asked advice from her pastor. When he recommended professional counseling, she delayed the appointment with a counselor, fearing what might be discovered. When she agreed, she was surprised when the counselor later pointed a finger of blame at her. *How could it be my fault?* she wondered. At the time, Anne could not realize that her unwillingness to look at the root cause had contributed to allowing the problem to persist.

Anne and Ginger showed up at my office in a desperation visit. As Anne described her daughter's behavior in detail, I realized Ginger's behavior was not consistent with a normal strong-willed child (although Ginger was definitely strong-willed). She was raised by two loving parents, whose younger son was as normal as American apple pie. As we spoke openly, it became obvious that Ginger was weaving for herself an emotional cocoon. She wanted no close friends, adult or peer. She consistently drove them away with violent behavior. Though only in the second grade, she was approaching one hundred pounds. Strong discipline did not work; it seemed she actually was begging for hard corporal punishment. When Anne would attempt to pray with her daughter, Ginger refused. She loathed church and would not participate in anything of a spiritual nature.

Later I spoke with both parents, describing an emotional cocoon and discussing how to respond to it. "Be prepared for what the cocoon contains," I said to Anne and

Brad as they both wept. "All the symptoms point to sexual molestation as the cause."

Ginger's immature emotions had been severely damaged. Perverted family members sometimes lurk in unsuspecting places. In Ginger's case it was a trusted uncle. Anne and Brad did their best to guard against it, but failed.

Ginger's emotional cocoon was the only place for comfort. As a result of her suppressed emotions, her relationships suffered by diverted anger, her spiritual life had been dying at the young age of seven, and she was neglecting herself physically. Ginger was off balance and in need of stabilized emotions. Each strand of the heritage cord had been thinned to become brittle and close to the breaking point.

This is a dangerous posture to find yourself in. Cocoons are dark places where anything can be buried. The trauma of emotional injury seeks out dark, damp spots within the cocoon in which to hide.

In case you think Ginger's response is unusual, realize that emotional cocooning is a normal human experience. Ginger's was extreme, of course, but we all like to hide in cocoons to a certain extent. Protective cocoons are particularly tempting when our emotions become fragile. Spend time with any group of children and you can pick out almost immediately the ones who are wearing a protection for their emotions. They only reveal a portion of how they feel in a crowd until they can survey the intent and direction of that group of people. When they feel comfortable, then they allow more of themselves to be exposed. But any time those emotions are stepped on they will withdraw them promptly.

Inside that cocoon we will put things that we feel we must hide. For Ginger, she had within her cocoon the hurt of molestation. She feared men. She dwelt on the harm, she dreamed of the harm, but she would not share it with anyone. So she evidenced suppression aggression: The suppression of the injury manifested itself in aggressive behavior. Accompanying the aggression were stages of deep depression and heightened anxiety. All these foul symptoms came from within her cocoon. They manifested themselves because there just wasn't room for all of it inside, so it showed up in the strangest places.

Suppressed emotions are like an inflated beach ball being pushed under the water. Try pushing a beach ball one foot under the water in a swimming pool. It's impossible to keep the ball below the surface for very long. It will escape from under your control and resurface in another area of the pool, no matter how much pressure you exert on it from the top. When we attempt to push an emotional problem below the surface, or when spiritual or social conflict remains unresolved, those problems will slip from under your control and manifest themselves somewhere else. It is then that we will see the problem manifested.

We were witnessing this reality with Ginger. Her suppressed emotional trauma was rearing its ugly head through both spiritual and relational conflict. Fortunately, we were able to trace the symptoms to their root cause and begin working to repair her damaged stabilizer bar. How? By giving her a safe, loving environment in which to deal with her pain.

REPAIRING THE STABILIZER BAR

I worked with Ginger's parents to help them begin the repair process. Their daughter's emotional stabilizer bar had been weakened. We identified several action points. If your (or your child's) emotions have been suppressed and suppression aggression seems to be showing, I recommend the same action plan.

1. RECOGNIZE AND DIVERT THE PAIN

With Ginger's emotions having been so severely damaged, it was necessary to recognize and divert the impact of her emotional pain. Notice that I did not say divert her *attention* from the pain, but divert the *pain itself* onto the stronger elements of her heritage baton—the spiritual and relational. How? First, inject a strong sense of acceptance, demonstrated through relationship with the family.

For Ginger, her mom, dad, and brother worked to create an environment of understanding and safety. In that setting Ginger could recuperate from the trauma that her fragile emotions had endured. Her family watched for the "warning signs" and reacted in love. Whether she was tired, angry, lonely, or confused, they responded with a healthy heaping of relational support. They made every effort during those early days of healing to protect her from any unnecessary emotional traffic. In short, they created a temporary detour so that God could begin repairing the damage.

2. REPAIR THE DAMAGE

Second, repair the damage. Only God can truly repair the damage of emotional trauma; yet we can lend a hand by consistently demonstrating and reinforcing what is true. Whether it is divorce, alcoholism, or, like Ginger, sexual abuse, a child hurt by emotional trauma will be bombarded by lies that undermine the ability to see truth clearly. Lies such as:

"You deserved it because you're a bad girl."

"You can't trust anybody, not even Mom or Dad."

"The molestation (divorce, rejection by a friend, etc.) was your fault."

"This pain will never end."

During such accusing times we must stand eye to eye with the truth. After all, God does not heal with deceit; He only heals with truth. To pretend the incident never happened or to sugar coat the problem is not the solution. Sadly, that is exactly how most families deal with an emotional hit.

Fortunately for Ginger, she was allowed to face the truth, and healing has begun. The truths she recognized are truths that should exist in every family. Truths such as:

- She is totally and unconditionally accepted.

- Most people can be trusted, especially Mom and Dad.

- Healing will come.

- The trauma was not her fault.

- No one deserves what she went through. God does not give us such trauma to punish us.

- God does care, and hates what happened to her.

As Ginger and her parents have discovered, when the truth is spoken, lies are broken. And when lies are broken, the emotional stabilizer bar will be repaired.

This same process is vital regardless of the specific source of pain. The need to repair the damage caused by divorce, the death of a loved one, betrayal by a close friend, peer rejection, or any other such "hit" is part of what a healthy emotional legacy will provide. Remember, even if your child has not suffered a major emotional trauma, providing her (or him) with unconditional acceptance, consistent, trustworthy actions, and a proper image of a caring God can give her a stable emotional legacy that can sustain her when the emotional trauma does come.

3. GIVE YOUR CHILD A PLACE OF REST, NOT RESCUE

Perhaps the most difficult aspect of helping our children repair their stabilizer bar is avoiding the desire to rescue them. Everything within us wants to protect them from every pain. But as Ginger's parents discovered, that is impossible. It is also harmful.

Our natural desire is to rescue our children, protecting them from all emotional pain. But we must be careful. There are some things that our children must struggle through to mature. Our responsibility is to give them a safe place to learn and a loving environment in which emotional maturity can grow. If we repeatedly shield them from all harm, they will remain weak. We must somehow find the balance between providing a nurturing, safe environment in which to rest from life's struggles and building a wall of protection to escape from them. The former nurtures growth. The latter can create emotional cripples.

Your child's ability to mature emotionally is like a caterpillar maturing into a butterfly. Joe, a friend of mine, took a long walk one day and spotted a cocoon attached to a tree branch. He looked closely and thought a violent confrontation was taking place inside the caterpillar's temporary home. The cocoon was twitching vigorously. Joe wondered if an intruder or a predator was stealing the cocoon for lunch. He got closer still to the cocoon and could see through the translucent covering a tightly packed butterfly struggling wildly to free itself.

Joe watched for a few minutes. Then he felt his heart go out to the poor floundering creature. So he reached out and ripped open the remaining area of the cocoon for the butterfly to be relieved of the writhing. His intentions were good. But his assistance forever crippled the butterfly.

Joe did not know that through the struggle the butterfly was strengthening its wings. As the fragile creature struggled in the difficult process of breaking free, it exercised its furled wings, pumping blood into the two appendages. The butterfly prepares for flight by his furious and wearying process of pumping its wings. Sadly, Joe's efforts had served to doom the very life he intended to save.

We must not rescue our children from their every crisis; part of growing up demands that they learn to deal with crises themselves. But we can and should help them by providing a refuge when they come to us and help if they ask. This is how our children mature into independent, strong adults.

LEADING INDICATORS FOR AN EMOTIONAL LEGACY

Clearly, a strong emotional legacy offers a stabilizing influence for our children. We conclude our look at what constitutes a strong legacy by looking at the leading indicators for an emotional legacy. What should we strive for, and what should we avoid in the process of creating an environment of love and security?

A STRONG EMOTIONAL LEGACY . . .

- Provides a safe environment in which deep emotional roots can grow.

- Fosters confidence through stability.

- Conveys a tone of trusting support.

- Nurtures a strong sense of positive identity.

- Creates a "resting place" for the soul.

- Demonstrates unconditional love.

A WEAK EMOTIONAL LEGACY . . .

- Breeds insecurity and shallow emotional development.

- Fosters fearfulness through instability.

- Conveys a tone of mistrust, criticism, or apathy.

- Undermines a healthy sense of personal worth.

- Causes inward turmoil.

- Communicates that a person doesn't measure up.

Such a comparison is not designed to discourage those who had more weak than strong in their legacy. Nor is the intent to drive us to point an accusing finger at our parents. The past is the past, and it cannot be changed. It can, however, show us how to create a strong emotional legacy for our children, and show us where we are now in passing a healthy emotional legacy on to our children.

EVALUATING YOUR LEGACY

Were you given a strong or a weak emotional legacy? As with the spiritual legacy evaluation in the previous chapter, take a few minutes to complete the Emotional Legacy Evaluation.

As you answer the following questions, note that a strong emotional legacy is even more rare than a solid spiritual legacy for several reasons. First, there is no "Users Manual" for parents on how to create an environment which fosters the positive characteristics we've identified. Second, even if there were, emotions are tricky things, and we vary from person to person in how we experience the circumstances of life. Two people who grew up in the same family might score their legacy on opposite ends of the spectrum, depending upon the personal dynamics and tendencies involved. Finally, we are all prone toward failure. Intentionally or not, most parents, including yours, will err to one extreme or the other, producing a less than balanced home environment.

The key question is not whether or not your emotional legacy was perfect, but what characteristics you would like to build into the legacy you pass to others. Even if you miss the mark in some ways, setting the right target is an important first step.

By the way, Ginger's situation has turned around. The path her parents are taking is helping her break free from the cocoon. I am reminded of the Detroit airport plane crash and Cecilia Cichan. For Ginger, I hear once more those beautiful words: She is expected to recover!

Emotional Legacy Evaluation

Answer each question by circling the number that best reflects the legacy you have received from your parents; then add your total score.

1. When you walked into your house, what was your feeling?
    1—Dread
    2—Tension
    3—Chaos
    4—Stability
    5—Calm
    6—Warmth

2. Which word best describes the tone of your home?
    1—Hateful
    2—Angry
    3—Sad
    4—Serious
    5—Relaxed
    6—Fun

3. What was the message of your family life?
    1—You are worthless.
    2—You are a burden.
    3—You are OK.
    4—You are respected.
    5—You are important.
    6—You are the greatest.

4. Which word best describes the "fragrance" of your home life?
    1—Repulsive
    2—Rotten
    3—Unpleasant
    4—Sterile
    5—Fresh
    6—Sweet

5. Which was most frequent in your home?
    1—An intense fight
    2—The silent treatment
    3—Detached apathy
    4—A strong disagreement
    5—A kind word
    6—An affectionate hug

Results
Above 24 = Strong emotional legacy
  19–24 = Healthy legacy
  14–18 = Mixed legacy—good and bad elements
  10–13 = Weak emotional legacy
Below 10 = Damaged emotional legacy

Chapter Five

YOUR SOCIAL LEGACY

A s our children were growing up, Gail and I tried to give them the security of knowing that we were setting boundaries for them. They had limits beyond which they could not go, but within those boundaries they had much freedom. We set perimeters for almost every area of their lives. That was our responsibility. One of the most difficult challenges in that process was setting clearly defined borders on relationships. Proper relationships are important, both within the family and with friends outside the home.

Your relationships during the childhood years contribute to your social legacy, and nowhere are proper social interaction and relationship demonstrated better than in the home. Here you learned—and your own children will learn—lessons about respect, love, courtesy, and involvement.

For instance, when our son Matt was seven, he learned an important lesson about respect from his interactions with his mother and me. My wife is not a "wait till your father gets home" type of mom. She responds now to what is taking place and, as a result, has excellent control of the home. One day, though, Matt thought it was time to challenge "good ol' Mom," and Gail was having a very difficult time with his strong will. I heard him say something to his mother, and more than Matt's words, I heard his sharp tone of disrespect. I decided to put myself in the middle of the confrontation.

"Son, she may be your mom, but she is my wife. I don't allow anyone to talk to my wife like that, and I won't allow you to, either." Immediately his attitude changed. When he realized that his mother and I were in this episode together, that we were on the same side—against his rotten attitude—his posture changed.

As a matter of fact, he never gave his mother that kind of trouble again. He saw us unified. He realized that to defy one of us was to defy us both, an important point for kids to understand.

A few weeks later my wife and I were in our bedroom having an intense disagreement over some unimportant issue. Each of us felt strongly about our own particular position. I explained to her in a "no uncertain" tone of voice my position. Just then, Matt stuck his head in the doorway, focused his eyes on me, and said playfully, "She may be your wife, but she is my mom and . . ." I think he got the point—and so did I!

WHAT IS A SOCIAL LEGACY?

Perhaps the most difficult component of the legacy baton to grab a hold of is the social. Passing on a strong social legacy is a challenge, because our social nature is a complex mixture of what we do and who we are. Part of the complexity arises from the many variables existing within family relationships; the remainder comes from the social relationships outside the family.

Here's a definition of the social legacy:

A social legacy is giving the child the insight and strong social skills for cultivating healthy, stable relationships.

As they mature, children must learn to relate to family members, friends, peers, teachers, and eventually co-workers, the boss, customers, the banker, the butcher, and the baker. Like it or not, relating well to others is vital to the process of living. And for better or worse, the primary classroom of relational competence is the home, which is why it is so critical that we understand the importance of passing a solid relational legacy to our children.

If you want to see your children run a successful business, don't just train them in finance or management. Teach them about people. If you want them to become great teachers, don't simply educate them in the three R's. Teach them about people. If you want them to rise above the odds, don't just make them tough. Teach them about people. The most significant skill you can give your child is not academic prowess or business savvy. It is the fine art of relating to people.

The guru of relational competence, Dale Carnegie, put it like this:

> Dealing with people is probably the biggest problem you face, especially if you are in business. Yes, and that is also true if you are a housewife, architect or engineer. Research done a few years ago under the auspices of the Carnegie Foundation for the Advancement of Teaching uncovered a most important and significant fact—a fact later confirmed by additional studies made at the Carnegie Institute of Technology. These investigations revealed that even in such technical lines as engineering, about 15 percent of one's financial success is due to one's technical knowledge and about 85 percent is due to skill in human engineering—to personality and the ability to lead people.[1]

Those who learn to relate well to others have an edge in the game of life. Those who don't are doomed to mediocrity at best, and failure at worst.

Clearly, a strong social legacy is a great gift to our child. And the strength of this legacy depends, as do the spiritual and emotional components, on our modeling as parents. Consider your own parents. If you grew up in a family that avoided conflict at all costs, you may become a doormat. If your parents tried to influence each other through shouting matches and manipulation, as an adult you may find yourself using similar approaches, driving others away. Whatever the pattern may have been, it tends to show up in present and future relationships.

Of course, as adults we can change the pattern. We have the capacity and responsibility to grow beyond the foundation we were given. Still, it is much easier to cultivate healthy relationships today if we saw them modeled yesterday. That is why it is important that we model strong relationships to our children.

BUILDING BLOCKS

Many of us never saw good relationships in our own home while growing up, and have little context for becoming a proper model today. What are some of the foundational building blocks to a solid social legacy? Although many could be cited here, four factors stand out as vital. Model these before your children, and you are on your way to building a solid social legacy.

1. RESPECT

As we saw in chapter 3, Billy had a weak spiritual legacy, which contributed to his anger and foul speech. But his appetite for stealing, brawling, and abusing his wife came directly from his lack of a solid social legacy. Neither his father nor his mother had any desire to build a relationship with their son. They did not respect him . . . they did not respect each other . . . they really did not even respect themselves. As a result, Billy inherited disrespect—disrespect for others, including his own wife, whom he said he loved.

Respect begins within each individual and works its way out to others. If I do not respect myself, I certainly have no reason to respect anyone else. If I do not respect my possessions, I will not respect the possessions of others. Billy respected nothing and nobody, so his lack of respect led him to take anything belonging to anybody.

There is a reason that God told Adam to "keep and dress" the garden. We develop a healthy respect for that which we put effort into. Adam could sit back after a hard day of work in the garden and appreciate his efforts. That time of reflection created within him a deepening desire to build and not tear down. Adam established a relationship to his property that taught him to appreciate the effort someone else may put into his property.

Billy never learned that principle. He told me, "What I possessed I got without ever trying. I never needed to sit at the end of a day and reflect on what I had accomplished. In fact, I mocked and laughed at those I had duped and ripped off."

At an early age this element in the social should be taught. A healthy respect for self will help our children to develop their own talents. Respect for property will ward off vandalism and stealing. Respect for their own bodies will help them respect the person of others. Morality moves to the forefront when our children learn their bodies are not to be instruments of pleasure and self-gratification (1 Corinthians 6:18–20).

We will discuss how to foster an environment of respect among our children in chapter 7, where we examine the family fragrance.

2. RESPONSIBILITY

Respect leads to responsibility, the second factor in creating a social legacy. Respect fosters responsibility. If I respect my right to ownership, then I take on the responsibility of caring for what I own, and I realize and respect the responsibility for what others possess. Conversely, remove respect and the resulting desire to be responsible for what we have, and a different *R* enters the equation: We begin to scream about "rights." When we do not treat our surroundings with a healthy respect . . . when we do not want to take on responsibility, then the easiest word to grab for is our "rights." The breakdown of respect and responsibility has led our nation into a wasteland where everyone is yelling for his rights. We hold marches, we attend rallies, we scan the legal system for loopholes, we all want our rights.

If anyone had a reason to claim his rights, it was Jim, the young man at Becky's wedding. His father left the family to follow after sensual pleasures while Jim was still very young. His mother reacted by turning inward, becoming consumed with her own loneliness and suffering, leaving Jim to practically raise himself. Nobody in his family would take on the responsibility of passing a heritage down to him. Jim had the "right" to continue a negative, self-centered pattern. After all, life had gypped him out of a healthy family.

Jim could have given up, made wrong choices, thrown responsibility and respect to the wind, and demanded his set of rights, but he didn't. He didn't major on rights; he majored on responsibility and respect.

Today, Jim is a model of responsible manhood for his wife, young son, and others. The cycle has been broken, all because Jim refused to claim his "rights" and accepted his responsibility. Someone accurately observed that if we have the Statue of Liberty on the East Coast, maybe we should erect a "Statue of Responsibility" on the West Coast . . . for without responsibility spanning our nation, liberty means nothing. If you have any doubt, just ask Jim.

We can impart responsibility to our children by teaching them respect for themselves and by assigning them duties within the family. Such responsibilities will give your children a chance to show themselves their value and fill a key role within the family. Duties also allow them to learn to be accountable for their actions.

Of course, such duties do not rule out your children's making wrong choices once in a while. Give them room to make mistakes. After all, it is when we are allowed to make mistakes or to fail that we are taught wisdom, values, and the stewardship of responsibility.

3. LOVE AND ACCEPTANCE

As parents, often we need to let our children suffer the consequences of inappropriate behavior. Letting our children face the consequences can teach them both respect and responsibility. Yet this is often difficult to do because we fail to distinguish unconditional love of the person from conditional acceptance of behavior. Parents should verbalize and demonstrate love to their children with no strings attached. Such love, the kind that says "I love you no matter what," contributes to strong, healthy relationships with family members, friends, and coworkers.

What's the difference between unconditional love of the person and conditional acceptance of behavior? Kurt has clarified this distinction in his book *Responsible Living in an Age of Excuses:*

> I love my son unconditionally. No matter what he does throughout his lifetime, I will love him. However, there will be times when I will be unable to accept his behavior. Because I love him, I will discipline wrong actions and attitudes. Yet, my conditional acceptance of his choices will not detract from my unconditional love of his person. As long as I consistently demonstrate both, Kyle will grow up understanding that Dad loves him too much to let him do whatever he wants.[2]

Kurt noted that God deals with His own children in the same manner. He demonstrates unconditional love by providing salvation for all (Romans 5:8), yet He demonstrates conditional acceptance by disciplining sinful behavior (Hebrews 12:6).

Similarly, in our relationships with our children—and in every healthy relationship—we must balance unconditional love with conditional acceptance of behavior. We should expect our children to obey because it is what's right; and because we love them so fully, we want what is right for them. When they disobey, we should not hold them back from the natural consequence of their wrongful behavior. As Kurt wrote,

> Although it is impossible to prevent those we love from making foolish or sinful choices, we can allow them to suffer the consequences of their behavior. When we protect others from the consequences of foolish living, we prevent their maturation, and ensure continued folly. If they burn themselves, however, they may realize the danger of playing with matches. And we may prevent a forest fire.[3]

Part of giving a solid relational legacy includes making sure our kids know they are totally, unconditionally loved. But at the same time, we must be certain they realize that some behaviors will not be accepted. One way to do this is to establish and enforce rules in the context of a loving, supportive relationship.

4. BORDERS

Setting borders is not just helpful for a strong relationship; it is essential for the social welfare of our children. A Minnesota Crime Commission report offered this assessment of children and deliquency:

> Every baby starts life as a little savage. He is completely selfish and self-centered. He wants what he wants when he wants it: his bottle, his mother's attention, his playmate's toy, his uncle's watch. Deny these and he seethes with rage and aggressiveness, which would be murderous were he not so helpless. This means that ALL children, not just certain children, are born delinquent. If permitted to continue in the self-centered world of infancy, given free reign to his impulsive actions, every child would grow up a criminal, a thief, a killer, a rapist.[4]

The implication of the above finding is this: We as parents have only eighteen years to civilize our children and prepare them to be released into society as productive citizens. We must avoid the temptation to "cop out" of our responsibilities. Some parents have settled for the instant, immediate, easy way. They shirk their responsibility and become derelict.

We must not renounce our duties as some have, claiming the challenge is too demanding. Instead we must set up social boundaries, even though social borders are not easily taught and we will face resistance. The security and stability of our children are too important.

Social borders should include how our children should relate to God, as well as to authority, their peers, their environment, and their siblings.

Drive toward the mountain range just west of Colorado Springs, and you will soon encounter Pikes Peak. This imposing mountaintop, more than 14,000 feet tall, towers over the city below, and many tourists love to reach the summit, a gateway to the Rocky Mountains.

You can get there several ways: by hiking, biking, taking a cog wheel train, even via an annual road race. Most choose to go via car, from the foothills all the way to the top. But driving Pikes Peak Highway poses one distinct problem: the narrow highway has no protective siderail. If you accidently swerve too far right, you are guaranteed a quick trip back to the bottom of the mountain. There is nothing to clearly mark the borders, so the trip is either avoided or undertaken with great care. It is not the most carefree of journeys.

The same applies when it comes to relational borders. Kids need to be instructed in, and have the opportunity to observe, very clear borders. The journey to adulthood is not carefree; it requires continual effort on your part, and there are ruts along the way. But the outcome—a gorgeous view at the top (to be enjoyed by both you and your children)—makes the effort to construct and maintain the borders worthwhile.

Here are some of the questions our children will need to answer on their journey to adulthood. They are excellent questions for parents to ask their children as well as themselves. They will help you to establish proper boundaries in your home that every member can learn to respect. The right answers to the following questions will come when your spouse and you have set clear and consistent boundaries for your children (and observe them in your own relationship with each other):

- How far can I go in challenging authority before I've crossed the line into disrespect?

- How should I respond when I am treated unfairly?

- How important is my tone of voice when I talk to my parents and others?

- When, if ever, is losing my temper appropriate?

- Where do my rights end and the rights of others begin?

- Is it ever right to fight?

- How should I react when others are treated wrongly?

The list could go on and on. The home is the place such questions should be answered—where the borders should be established. Doing so gives children a protective side-rail, allowing them to enjoy the journey rather than fear every dangerous curve.

RULES WITHIN RELATIONSHIP

As you set borders, keep one caution in mind. Because they are typically expressed as rules, borders are respected best when they are given with love. Jason, for example, learned right from wrong while growing up. But the moment he became old enough to make his own decisions, he rejected most of the values Mom and Dad had taught. What went wrong?

The primary reason was that rules were given in a relational vacuum. Jason's parents gave the right medicine, but it wasn't served with the spoonful of sugar, namely, strong relationship. For whatever reasons, they were distant. They loved Jason but had a hard time demonstrating it. Honest, open communication was difficult, so it rarely occurred. Jason was not given a forum in which to discuss, ask, question, or challenge Mom and Dad's "list." The inevitable result? Rebellion.

Boundaries must be set for children to grow, feel secure, and have direction. But they must come within a relationship. Rules without compassion and love become harsh taskmasters and can be misunderstood. We must show love.

Adam was given rules, including the prohibition of eating from a certain tree in the Garden, but he was not left to simply obey some cold set of mandates. They were given in the context of relationship with the rule-giver Himself. Similarly, the Israelites were given a set of rules, the Ten Commandments. They were warned about the need to keep them, but, as with Adam, they were not just left to obey some cold, unreachable rules. As God had walked and talked with Adam in the cool of the day, so He dwelt with Israel in a pillar of cloud and fire and spoke through Moses, a personal leader. The thing that God wanted from and for both Adam and the Jewish nation was a relationship. He knew how important that was to their well-being.

Today God desires a relationship with each of us. He did not just open the back window of heaven and holler out some vague instructions as to how we can live this life and prepare for eternity. He sent His Son to show us He knows our frame and is acquainted with our weaknesses, then He sent His Holy Spirit to indwell us, to bear witness with us, that the relationship will continue. We may break the rules, but we can't sever the relationship. It is that relationship with the Creator that makes us, out of love, heed the rules.

You see, rules without a relationship usually lead to rebellion.

If parents have a set of rules that are force-fed to the children, and the rules are not buffered with a family relationship, a relationship of worth where legitimate questions can be discussed, then rebellion is fostered, and rights are demanded. On the other hand, if the same family has the same set of rules that are polished by a warm, unconditional, accepting relationship, respect is fostered and responsibility is accepted.

THE LEADING INDICATORS
FOR A SOCIAL LEGACY

Once again, a strong social legacy provides the foundation for cultivating healthy, stable relationships. We've touched upon several aspects of this process already. Let's briefly list some of the leading indicators we should be instilling in our own children before evaluating the social legacy we've inherited.

A STRONG SOCIAL LEGACY . . .

- Sets clear "borders" on how to appropriately treat others.

- Teaches respect for all people.

- Instills a sense of responsibility for the feelings and property of others.

- Balances unconditional love for the person with conditional acceptance of behavior.

- Enforces rules in the context of a loving relationship.

- Models clear and sensitive communication skills.

A WEAK SOCIAL LEGACY . . .

- Causes confusion regarding what is appropriate treatment and what is not.

- Treats others with disrespect.

- Follows a "survival of the fittest" perspective.

- Accepts wrong behavior in the name of love.

- Is dictatorial, enforcing rules for their own sake.

- Models poor interpersonal communication.

Which of the two extremes is closer to reality for you at this time? More important, which represents what you want to give from this day forward?

EVALUATING YOUR LEGACY

Let's take a look at the social legacy you were given in order to evaluate the relative strength of this element of your baton. Complete the Social Legacy Evaluation on the next page, remembering that, like the evaluations in the two previous chapters, this exercise is designed to help focus your attention on both the good and bad elements of your heritage. No one received a perfect heritage. In fact, if you score well on even one or two of the three, you beat the odds. Sadly, a strong heritage is the exception, not the norm.

Here's a final reminder as you consider your legacy evaluation scores in chapters 3–5. If one or two of the scores are very weak, don't give up on your ability to pass along a new, stronger heritage in place of the one you received. Some feel if part of their heritage is weak, they must reject the whole thing.

Remember Sarah? She was given a wonderful spiritual heritage, yet she rejected it. Why? Because her relational legacy was weak, driving her to rebellion. Unable to distinguish one strand of the cord from another, she rejected it all. Bad move on her part!

Frank, on the other hand, was given a terrific relational and emotional legacy, but left them behind. Why? Because his parents failed to give him a spiritual foundation. So, when he became a Christian as a young adult, he began viewing everything his parents did as substandard. That is unfortunate. His parents did a great job on two aspects of the heritage. Frank should have kept the good and built upon it, rather than reject it all.

The point is this: While it is dangerous to overly divide the spiritual, emotional, and relational aspects of our heritage, it can also be helpful. It allows us to identify and replace the bad, while keeping and building upon the good. And remember, many of us received some of both.

And even if we didn't, all of us can start afresh today!

Social Legacy Evaluation

Answer each question by circling the number that best reflects the legacy you have received from your parents; then add your total score.

1. Which television family most closely resembles the social tone of your own?

>   1—"Married . . . with Children"
>   2—"Roseanne"
>   3—"The Simpsons"
>   4—"The Wonder Years"
>   5—"Home Improvement"
>   6—"The Cosby Show"

2. What was the message of your home life with regard to relationships?

>   1—"Step on others to get your way."
>   2—"Hurt them if they hurt you."
>   3—"Demand your rights."
>   4—"Mind your own business."

5—"Treat others with respect."
6—"Put others before yourself."

3. How were rules set and enforced in your home?
1—Independent of relationship
2—In reaction to parental stress
3—Dictatorially
4—Inconsistently
5—Out of concern for my well-being
6—In the context of a loving relationship

4. Which word best characterizes the tone of communication in your home?
1—Shouting
2—Manipulation
3—Confusing
4—Clear
5—Constructive
6—Courteous

5. How did your family deal with wrong behavior?
1—Subtle reinforcement
2—Accepted in the name of love
3—Guilt trip
4—Severe punishment
5—Discussion
6—Loving, firm discipline

Results
Above 24 = Strong social legacy
  19–24 = Healthy legacy
  14–18 = Mixed legacy—good and bad elements
  10–13 = Weak social legacy
Below 10 = Damaged social legacy

Chapter Six

CHOOSING WHAT YOU WILL WEAR

S hari, a beautiful young lady in her twenties, did not like the spotlight too much, yet she could perform on stage with the most talented and contribute tons of support. I will never forget her big, beautiful dark eyes, and her toothy, white smile that could win any heart. Shari let me in on a secret one day as we worked together toward the completion of a project for a Christmas drama.

"I'm going to begin searching for my dad," she said.

"What?" I asked in disbelief. "I know your dad. I see him at church once in a while."

"He is my stepdad," Shari said, setting things straight. "My real dad is a tennis star. A very popular star in his day," she remarked, her big eyes flashing. "I'm the product of a 'one-night stand' between him and my mom . . . I have to find him."

My face wore the shock of the information as she unfolded her life in front of me. Near the end of her story, tears as big as pearls dropped from her eyes.

She did begin to search, and when she got close to the star, she was repelled, rejected just as she was at birth. Shari's mom tried to give her daughter as much as she could, but the pressures of trying to make it on her own caused her to forsake motherhood for her own personal security. Shari suffered through it. She was handed a pile of rags to wear as her heritage. She refused to settle for rags. Instead, at a very early age, she began to sew for herself that beautiful gown. At this very moment, she and her husband are passing that heritage to their three young children.

In the introduction, my wife, Gail, contrasted some shredded rags with an elegant wedding gown and asked, "What were you handed? Were you handed rags? If so, are you content to continue wearing them?" Gail said we can "reject the rags and begin to sew an exquisite gown for our children." Such a gown can be yours. Or, as a man, you can trade in your rags for a royal robe.

PUTTING ON RAGS

Another option is available, though. Gail noted that we can take off the gown or robe we received from our parents and clothe ourselves in rags. That's what Sarah did. Though handed a wonderful heritage, she chose to reject it. You may recall her reaction to the wedding ceremony described in chapter 1—mocking this "heritage bunk" as a joke . . . "pie in the sky." And yet, no one could have been handed a better opportunity to handle the "passing of the heritage baton" than she. Sarah's parents taught her truth, gave her love, kept her safe, and did all they could to give her an edge in the game of life. But she rejected it all. Her parents were too devout for her taste. Wearing that sort of "gown" was not in vogue, and she wanted no part of it. Instead she made a sad and silly choice—riches to rags.

If you are like me, Sarah's story will disturb you. But what we parents must understand is that our children are not hollow mannequins. They are not marionettes on a string that we can pull at will. We must model a strong legacy. We must do our best. But our children are individuals—sinners like us—who are free to choose whether or not they will wear the legacy given. We are only responsible for the process. God must work directly on the child, who is responsible for the final product. Our child may leave a strong heritage behind—and many will.

OUR CHOICE

But before our children choose, we must. We can either choose to wear the Victorian gown (or royal robe) . . . or the rags. If you were fortunate enough to have been handed a gown or robe, then you must choose to wear it and pass it on. If you were passed rags, you can choose to discard them and begin sewing a gown. Contrary to popular opinion, none of us are complete victims of our past. All of us can break the generational cycle and launch a new day for ourselves and those we love. But how?

HOW TO BREAK THE GENERATIONAL CYCLE

As you finish Part 1, it's time to combine the three legacy evaluations into a course of action that can break the generational cycle. A course of action that can change rags to robes and gowns. We recommend three steps: look back, look up, and look ahead.

STEP ONE: LOOKING BACK

An honest evaluation of the heritage you were given is the first step toward choosing what you will wear. So take a hard look at your evaluations at the conclusion of chapters 3–5. Review your scores and then complete the Personal Heritage Survey below.

Personal Heritage Survey

This exercise is designed to help you identify the relative strength of the heritage you were given. As you answer the following questions, try to identify the good to keep, the bad to discard, and the weak to strengthen.

1. Drawing from the earlier evaluations, rate the general strength of each component of your heritage.

Spiritual Legacy:

STRONG HEALTHY MIXED WEAK DAMAGED

Emotional Legacy:

STRONG HEALTHY MIXED WEAK DAMAGED

Social Legacy:

STRONG HEALTHY MIXED WEAK DAMAGED

2. Starting with the strongest of the three components, list several characteristics that best summarize your leading legacy indicators. (You may want to review the lists in chapter 3, 4, and 5. Although your descriptions may be different, they may give you some general direction.)

My Spiritual Legacy   *Good or Bad?*

_____   _____

_____   _____

_____   _____

_____   _____

_____   _____

My Emotional Legacy   *Good or Bad?*

_____   _____

_____   _____

_____   _____

_____   _____

_____   _____

My Social Legacy   *Good or Bad?*

_____   _____

_____   _____

_____   _____

_____   _____

_____   _____

3. Finally, record any additional thoughts which could describe the heritage you were given. What things do you

appreciate about your home life? What things cause the most pain? What things have you taken for granted over the years? What negative issues may be impacting your attitudes and behaviors today? Take a few moments to contemplate these questions.

Now that you have spent some time looking back, you are ready to move on to step two in our process of choosing what you will wear: looking up.

STEP TWO: LOOKING UP

The process of honest evaluation will lead many to the realization, some for the first time, that they have unresolved issues to confront. Someone to forgive. Something to release. Fears to overcome. Bitterness to confess. You may recognize painful truths you should acknowledge or personal weaknesses to admit. Whatever the issues, deal with them once and for all. Don't allow their cruel grip to keep you in bondage to your past.

You can be free. Look up. Seek the Lord for what you need. From God you can find:

- The grace to forgive and be forgiven.

- The strength to admit your weakness, and accept help where needed.

- The faith to accept what is true, even when your emotions betray reality.

- The confidence to give the Lord the reins of your life, especially during those times when you feel out of control.

Talk to the Lord about whatever is on your heritage list. Ask Him to help you deal with whatever you find there. Believe me, He is more than willing to lend a hand!

STEP THREE: LOOKING AHEAD

Once you have identified the reality of your past and invited the Lord to help you confront any unresolved issues, the changes can begin. It is time to create the pattern for the gown you hope to sew and the robe you plan to wear. The exercise "Designing Your Heritage" will help you to envision the heritage that you are seeking.

As you complete the exercise, remember the purpose is to identify a specific goal. The old expression is true: Those who aim for nothing are sure to hit it. But with the findings of this exercise you have a target you can really shoot for. Completing this exercise is an important step on the road to giving a positive heritage. First, you establish the target; then you envision a new future. And before long, you will be actively engaged in sewing that new garment.

Designing Your Heritage

This exercise is designed to help you identify the heritage you want to give. Drawing upon your responses in the Personal Heritage Survey, list those qualities you seek to give and receive.

First, identify the characteristics of the heritage you would like to give. Don't allow doubt or insecurity to hold you back. In the blanks below list what you want it to be, not what you think is realistic. (Again, you may find it helpful to reference the leading indicators listed in chapters 3, 4, and 5. But don't let our suggestions limit your design.)

Then, next to the characteristics that you intend to give, circle the letter "K" for "keep," because they were solid aspects of the heritage you were given. Next to those that you consider weak in your own heritage, circle the letter "S" for "strengthen." Finally, next to those items in your heritage that you want to change in some way to improve, circle the letter "C." This step will become important later as you build your heritage plan, helping you zero in on those areas requiring the most intentional effort.

The Spiritual Legacy I want to give: Category

_____ K   S   C

_____ K   S   C

_____ K   S   C

_____ K   S   C

_____ K   S   C

_____ K   S   C

The Emotional Legacy I want to give: Category

_____ K   S   C

_____ K   S   C

_____ K   S   C

_____ K   S   C

_____ K   S   C

_____ K   S   C

The Social Legacy I want to give: Category

_____ K   S   C

_____ K   S   C

_____ K   S   C

_____ K   S   C

_____ K   S   C

_____ K   S   C

A WAYWARD WOMAN

The Jewish woman brushes the sand from her face and tries to lift herself from the ground where the men had dumped her like household garbage. She remembers being with a man who had made an offer for her services. She was suspicious, but because the amount was so substantial (that's the way she made her living) she could survive for another couple of weeks without having to sell herself again. The man is not with her now, and she slowly rubs her hands together, knocking off the final residue of sand. As she does, another wave of nausea settles in the pit of her stomach.

No longer dazed, the wayward woman recognizes that the voices of a shouting mob that had once sounded at a distance actually are close and recognizable. The men standing over her are the same men who burst through the door of her apartment while she was with the suspicious man who had offered that stash of cash. . . . They're the leaders from the local synagogue! By the questions being volleyed back and forth over her, she realizes she has been set up. Her eyes hurriedly analyze the crowd. *That suspicious man, he isn't anywhere to be found. I'm here alone.*

CONDEMNATION

"This woman was caught in the very act," someone informs the crowd.

"Yeah, what should happen to her?"

"Moses' law says she should be stoned."

That statement sent chills down her back, and it hushes the crowd.

This is it, she says to herself. Death would be a welcome friend compared to the miserable life she had been living.

A shadow falls over her from a man kneeling in the dirt. He's drawing figures in the sand. *What is it he's making with his finger?* The silence is torture . . . then with a voice as soft as she has ever heard, he orders, "Whoever is without sin . . . cast the first stone."

She winces, waiting for the pain of the first rock to hit. The tension is breached by the crunching of sand underneath hurried sandals. She looks around in surprise. The crowd—everyone is leaving.

COMPASSION

"Your accusers, lady, where are they?"

For the first time she gathers enough courage to shake off the humiliation, and after a hasty glance around, she answers. "There are none."

"Neither do I condemn you," affirms Jesus. "Go away now . . . sin no more."

REMEMBERING YET CHANGING

Powerful words, but is it realistic to think she will sin no more? What about all the awful experiences she has that will remind her constantly about her past? When she sets foot outside her hut, the eyes of those who know who she is will be scowling, reminding her of a sordid past.

The thing we must remember is that Jesus' words to her, "Go away . . . don't sin anymore," did not mention forgetting. "Go away and forget" were not His words because He knows forgetting is impossible. We will remember the losses and hurts of our past.

For this woman it may have been rape or abuse. It certainly included the shame and guilt of a one-night stand, and perhaps years of unfaithfulness or even life as a prostitute. Such memories do not quickly disappear.

STARTING OVER

Though we know little about this woman,[1] she is not unlike many of us who have stumbled. Part of our stumbling comes from a poor spiritual, emotional, or social inheritance, part from our own sinful choices.

Remember, this woman was someone's precious child. All her desires began as normal, but somewhere in the wreckage of the dailyness of living, they got twisted. She lost sight of what truly mattered. Perhaps she followed in the footsteps, unknowingly, of a mom who lived the same lifestyle. Maybe she saw a dad who masked himself in every situation, except at home. His "religion" meant nothing to him and resulted in meaning even less to her. Just the sight of the synagogue was repulsive . . . and those hypocrites who prayed every day on the street corner at 9 A.M., 12 P.M., and 3 P.M. propelled her even farther into her contorted attitude.

At an early age, her natural feelings of love were awakened and interlaced with the abnormal . . . so where she found herself did not really seem so wrong . . . her experiences had anesthetized her . . . and so, she was cannon fodder for the religious sect who needed a pawn to trap Jesus.

Or perhaps not. Maybe her story was completely different, the other extreme. She was born in a home thick with love. She was the delight of a mom and the blissful joy of a father who beamed. Her father worked hard in the family business, not to have an impressive home and fields, but to give his child what he could not have.

She may have been educated in a private school . . . and had the finest clothes. She was awakened early on the Sabbath because Mom and Dad were true believers. Synagogue was not just another option; it was significant.

She could have been one who had every occasion to "know God" but simply chose to reject Him and what He represents.

Now, take both scenarios . . . stretch your imagination from the first extreme to the second. Where in that expanse do you find yourself?

"Nowhere," you may reply. Perhaps you say you have absolutely nothing in common with her.

Wait a second . . . yes, you do. We all do.

First, whether for good or bad, she was influenced by the heritage she was given. Past generations handed her something, and that something helped mold her life into what she became. The same is true for you and me.

Second, she had the freedom to choose. If her parents handed her rags to wear, she could have rejected them. If they handed her a wedding gown, she could wear it and pass that along. Or, like some, she could reject that gown and settle for rags.

We all make choices; we have that freedom. And we can all start over.

GIVE AND YOU WILL RECEIVE

If you were given a weak heritage, how can you get a strong one? The answer is simple, but profound. You get by giving. In the process of building a solid heritage for others, you also create one for yourself.

The Scriptures, at times, seem paradoxical. It goes against all rational reasoning to give something away so one might keep it. How is it that if one will "let go" he can be kept from falling? Shouldn't it be "hold tight" and climb as high as you can? Everybody knows that in order to get to the top and be successful one has to step on people's heads. What is this "consider others better than yourselves" (Philippians 2:3)? That's not sensible. Yet, when tried, it proves true.

Creating a heritage is much the same. It's humanly logical to think that giving a heritage to your children means just to buy it and keep it in a safety deposit box until the children are at the point in their lives to accept it. But that is not the way it works. The heritage is not free; it will cost you. But it also pays and pays and pays . . . when done right.

The value of the heritage is not in the keeping but in the giving. It's not an entitlement, but an inheritance ready to be given away. When you are busy building, giving, and passing it on to future generations, you may find that you yourself have received a heritage that you did not get from your parents. It is a heritage God has graced you with because of your diligence to your children and obedience to Him.

In Part 2, we will discuss some of the practical "how tos" of the heritage process. We will highlight the critical importance of creating an environment of love in the home, a sweet-smelling "family fragrance." We will also discuss "impression points" and how they can be used to influence our children with our values and character. Next, we will look at the process of establishing a clearly aligned "right angle" with our children, helping them understand what is normal, healthy living. We also will address the important role of family traditions. As each chapter concludes, you will be invited to evaluate your own heritage process to date, and commit to an action plan for making it better.

Now, let's open the tool chest and inspect the tools that will help us create an inheritance of love.

Part Two
THE HERITAGE TOOL CHEST

*Parents are not obligated to give their children
a secure future, but they are obligated to
give them a secure foundation on which
to build their own futures.*

Survey Bulletin

Chapter Seven

THE FAMILY FRAGRANCE

Whenever I smell one of several fragrances, I'm instantly transported back to my house as a child. The smell of homemade pies does it every time; so does the smell of hamburgers being cooked on the barbecue grill. The aroma of fresh coffee reminds me of the crisp, cool mornings at our north Texas home and my dad picking up his mug.

Today in our home Gail is a master of the beautiful fragrances that the senses can enjoy, and these bring their own memories as well as expectations. The smell of chocolate chip cookies or fudge cake baking in the oven, of onions frying in an open skillet, homemade potato/sausage soup simmering, or a pot roast that has lazily tenderized all day in the Crock-Pot. Each is enough to transport me quickly into "fantasy-fragrance land." All those particular aromas help me identify happy moments I can enjoy dwelling on in our family. Christmas has its own spiciness, Thanksgiving its sweet bounty of fresh fruit pies, and each reminds me of special family gatherings.

Family fragrances go deeper than the senses, however. They can have a lot to do with all three legacies, the emotional, spiritual, and social. If you were asked to explain the aromatic definition of your family legacies—if you had to describe them as memories—what words would you select? Would it be the spicy scent from a healthy exchange of differing opinions, coupled with mutual respect? Or would it be a pungent odor from a home's chaotic, criticizing, and uncaring atmosphere?

A Sweet Aroma

There are five key qualities to a healthy family fragrance, each contributing to an environment of love in the home. In fact, I call them The Fragrance Five. The first fragrance is demonstrative love—hugs, kisses, and all that wonderful mushy stuff. The second fragrance is giving each individual the respect he or she deserves. The third may be less obvious but equally important: creating a clear structure that keeps things organized. The fourth fragrance is the ability to laugh and have fun together. And the fifth sweet-smelling family fragrance relates to praising others, building them up, rather than tearing them down.

It's easy to remember The Fragrance Five; we can fit them into an acrostic using the word Aroma:

A	Affection
R	Respect
O	Order
M	Merriment
A	Affirmation

Thus the first item from our tool chest is actually a spice called aroma, a spice featuring five distinct fragrances that scent the home with love, creating an environment conducive to a positive heritage. Let's briefly examine the contribution of each fragrance to a loving home.

Fragrance One: Affection

Four-year-old Kyle pauses to contemplate how he will respond to his father's rather deep question, "What is love?" He knows Mommy and Daddy say it a lot, but what does it really mean? Finally, the answer comes. "It's when people hug and kiss each other all the time!" Not a bad summary.

THE POWER OF TOUCH

Affection certainly includes touching our children. In their excellent book *The Blessing*, Gary Smalley and John Trent offer a biblical model of parents blessing their children by giving them a strong sense of acceptance and identity. The first element Smalley and Trent identify is meaningful touch. They describe the power of affectionate touching in our lives, including two clinical studies that demonstrate the importance of touch.

> In a study at UCLA, it was found that just to maintain emotional and physical health, men and women need eight to ten meaningful touches each day! These researchers defined meaningful touch as a gentle touch, stroke, kiss or hug given by significant people in our lives (a husband or wife, parent, close friend, and so on). This study estimated that if some "type A driven" men would hug their wives several times each day, it would increase their life span by almost two years! (Not to mention the way it would improve their marriages.) Obviously, we can physically bless those around us (and even ourselves) with meaningful touch. . . .
>
> Researchers at the University of Miami Medical School's Touch Research Institute began giving premature babies forty-five minutes of massage each day. Within ten days, the massaged babies showed 47 percent greater weight gain than those children who were not regularly touched. In a second study, actual bone growth of young children who had been deprived of parental touching was half that of the bone growth of children who received adequate physical attention.[1]

Is there any doubt that displaying affection for those we love is a vital part of a strong heritage? Sure, we must say that we love them, but it is even better to show it. Touch is a tangible reminder of love. It feels good and it means much when we receive it, whether a hand on the shoulder, a rub on the back, or a warm kiss.

GIVING NURTURE

Demonstrative love was a theme of the apostle Paul in his teachings to the believers at Ephesus. After giving some strong instructions to husbands and wives, he turned his finger toward the fathers and made a pointed command. "Fathers," he said, "provoke not your children to wrath . . . but bring them up in the nurture and admonition of the Lord" (Ephesians 6:4, KJV). Two qualities are contained in that sentence: nurture and admonition. Admonishing our children is simply to counsel them against a fault, gently pointing to a blind spot in their character. It's an instruction to the children of their responsibilities. They will be held accountable for the consequences of not following them.

Nurturing, on the other hand, is the positive approach to leading our children to growth and features the love only we as parents can give them. Such love assures children that they are accepted by virtue of who they are, not what they do. And, being demonstrative, such love is shown them regularly.

Our children need to know they are accepted and loved. Through touch and words, we can dispense love like a treasure. You may not be able to give them every material thing they want, but you will grow them strong with the nurturing component of their family fragrance called affection. And love can be expressed in so many simple ways:

- Holding hands while walking through the mall

- A good-bye kiss in the morning before heading out the door

- A big bear hug when you get home

- Mom and Dad smooching in broad daylight!

- Saying "I love you, little buddy" just because you feel like it

- Calling your little daughter "baby doll" and watching her grin in shy reaction

These are the things that comprise demonstrative love. You know, all that wonderful mushy stuff. There's no need to make it more complicated than it is. Just show and tell others that you love and accept them.

FRAGRANCE TWO: RESPECT

Billy Graham was right: "A child who is allowed to be disrespectful to his parents will not have true respect for anyone." If there is anything that should be built into the fabric of every family, it is respect for the individual, starting with Mom and Dad. Not awe, reverence, or veneration, but an estimation in which we honor the worth of others. It is that respect due each family member simply because of who they are.

There are two types of respect we should reinforce at home. The first is entitled respect, and the second is earned respect.

ENTITLED RESPECT

Entitled respect is that which is commanded due to a person's position. "Honor your father and mother." There are no contingencies, no exceptions to this command. Just honor. The position entitles the holder (Ephesians 6). Respect those in government positions, because they are put there as ministers of God (Romans 13). Respect those who have the rule over you spiritually, and honor them (1 Timothy 5:17; Hebrews 13:7).

Children should understand this as well as see it modeled by their parents. If as an adult you denigrate entitled respect, how can you expect your children not to follow suit? How can a husband disrespect his wife, then as a father demand that the children respect his parental status? How can a wife disrespect her husband, then expect the kids to treat her right? How can parents "provoke children to wrath" and expect the kids to honor them in return?

EARNED RESPECT

This leads to our second category of respect, earned respect. Though entitled respect is drawn from who we are, earned respect comes from what we do. "Earned" is drawn from the concepts of "earnest" and "yearn." The primary purpose is to strive, implying an effort to advance or stretch forward. Earning respect is exactly that, a yearning to advance in all endeavors of the mind, body, social graces, and spirituality.[2] We gain it through our labor, our service to others, and our performance within the family unit. When we give due respect to those who are entitled to it, or have earned it, we, in the process, are preparing the way for respect to come back around our way. It is, indeed, a two-way avenue.

Respect fostered in the home will have a dramatic effect on all three areas of the heritage. Spiritually, it will give your child true value. Emotionally, it will give a sense of security. Socially, it will establish a foundation for treating others right.

FRAGRANCE THREE: ORDER

Hugs and kisses are great. Treating others with respect is essential. But if the home is unorganized and chaotic, it is impossible to create a sweet-smelling family fragrance. Like any other institution or organization, the home requires a setting of order and peace to be effective in the task of passing a solid heritage.

A SAFE AND PEACEFUL ENVIRONMENT

Our church runs a private school in Fresno, California. Recently, the students of the Senior Leadership Council were asked to respond to several questions to help guide the administration to improve educational quality. One of the survey questions asked what the students needed most from their instructors. Interestingly, a majority wrote, "The teacher should be in control." That was no surprise until later, in the presence of students, it was qualified. The students explained that it wasn't so much that they wanted the teacher in control of the classroom, as much as the teacher to be in control of him- or herself. They reasoned that if the teachers were in control of themselves, a safe and peaceful environment would automatically follow. The same is true in the home.

Many homes foster an atmosphere where the person who can yell the loudest or cry the most convincingly is in charge. Instead, the home should be a place of prevailing calm, a safe place that is emotionally restful. Someone must maintain control. Otherwise, an ordered, tranquil environment is impossible. Kurt was raised in a home of order, while his wife Olivia was not. He contrasts the impact of each.

"I grew up in a family of seven children. Here there was ample opportunity for confusion and stress. Seven kids screaming, teasing, fighting, and creating messes can quickly destroy any semblance of tranquillity. But my mother did a terrific job of creating and maintaining a sense of order at home. After a hard day of school, delivering papers, and playing pickup basketball, I knew I'd walk through the front door and be greeted to a home which was well organized and calm. It was generally a place of rest in the midst of an often hectic lifestyle.

"My wife, Olivia, on the other hand, had an entirely different experience. She was raised in a single-parent family of six children. Her mother was too busy and exhausted to maintain an ordered environment at home. As a result, chaos ruled. Olivia didn't return home to rest from the stress of life. She left her house to rest from the stress of home."

THE THREE R'S OF ORDER

The degree of order at home can make a difference in the heritage passing process. In order to create and maintain a proper environment, every home should include the three R's of order: rules, roles, and rights.

Rules. Without clear, well-defined rules in the home, anarchy is sure. Everyone must understand that certain actions are expected, while other behaviors will not be tolerated. The great experiment of permissive parenting has proven itself to be a major flop. Even Dr. Benjamin Spock, guru of permissive parenting advice during the fifties and sixties, has more recently recommended the need for firm discipline with children. In his words, "Parental firmness makes for a happier child."[3]

Children need clear borders established, giving them the security and self-confidence to become their best. As the parents of nine children, authors Linda and Richard Eyre write concerning children and security:

> Anarchy exists in a country or state without laws. The word conjures visions of confusion, rebellion, danger—not unlike what we often see and feel in our families. Legal systems not only protect our rights, our property, and our persons, they give us a stable, secure environment in which we can function and flourish. Ironically, our limits give us freedom, whereas, anarchy is the absence of both limits and freedom. Children come into the world and into our families needing and looking for limits and the security they give. When children are not given limits by their parents, they "push the envelope" farther and farther out, looking for boundaries that can give their life some meaning.[4]

To keep the home from becoming a place of anarchy, family rules are essential. Define them, write them down, communicate them, and stick to them. Here are three guidelines as you create the rules:

1. Keep the list short. The more rules, the less likely they will be remembered, let alone followed.

2. Don't major on the minors. If you devise a list of "nitpicky" rules about things that don't really matter, your family fragrance will have the scent of rigidity. Cover the important stuff, like treating others with respect, cleaning up after yourself, etc. But allow some room for flexibility on less substantial matters.

3. Be consistent. If you create a rule for one, it should apply to all. Age differences may alter the specific application of the rule from one child to the next, but the general principle should apply to everyone. By the way, that includes Mom and Dad!

Roles. Every member of the family has a role to play. But if those roles are not intentionally identified and clarified, then everyone will be forced (or will force someone) into a role that may not be appropriate or healthy. Mom and Dad, for example, must fill the vital roles of family authority. They are the executive, legislative, and judicial branches of the family government. Children, on the other hand, are citizens who have a voice in family affairs, but who must ultimately appeal to and submit to the direction of their leaders. Just as social anarchy occurs whenever there is a void in leadership, family anarchy will occur when Mom and Dad neglect to fill their role, or when little Johnny is allowed to resist their authority without consequence.

Many families have the form of such roles but fail to effectively carry out the associated responsibilities. Dad is absent in the name of earning a living. Mom passively allows the kids to take control in the name of unconditional love. The result? Chaos. The vacuum of authority drives the family into a "survival of the fittest" culture. The strongest personality takes over, whether the individual be a toddler with an attitude or a teenager with a mouth. Don't let that happen in your home. Establish clear roles for every family member, and then reinforce them in everyday life.

Rights. Once you've established clear rules and roles, be certain to guarantee every family member certain minimum rights. Everyone, for example, should have the right to be listened to. Your son and daughter should be able to voice their opinion as it relates to family affairs. Every family member should have a right to express concern over how they are treated, so long as it is done in a respectful tone.

After years of serving as a pastor in a church in Garland, Texas, Bill Sears was asked to accept a position coordinating the missions outreach of his denomination. The change represented a wonderful opportunity, but it also meant uprooting his family and moving them to another town. Respecting the rights of his teenage son to have a say in the matter, Pastor Sears told his son, Ron, about the offer.

"Your mother and I think it would be a good thing, but we realize that the move would have a serious impact upon you too. I want you to pray about the decision and let me know what you think we should do." He then said something that had a dramatic impact upon his boy. "Ronny, if you don't agree that we should go, we won't. You have the right to make this decision with us." Had Ronny's father forced the issue and ignored his son's right to participate in such a serious decision, Ronny may have rebelled—and certainly would have resisted. But thanks to a dad who understood and respected family rights, the move was made without a hitch, and Ronny learned a very important life lesson.

You see, where rights are not given, they will be demanded. And when rights are demanded, anarchy ensues. Give and guarantee your children "family rights" in order to foster a spirit of trust and mutual respect in the home. One way to give your children a platform to properly and respectfully present their feelings about rights is by holding weekly or monthly family meetings. Here their options can be exposed and carefully weighed. One family I know lives in a home where all the upstairs bedrooms converge on a small balcony overlooking the family room. Here Dad often calls a quick stand-up meeting to listen to all opinions before making a final decision.

Once again, order is a critical element to a positive family fragrance. Creating that sense of order requires establishing family rules, clarifying family roles, and guaranteeing family rights.

FRAGRANCE FOUR: MERRIMENT

A healthy dose of merriment in the home is good medicine. More than any other place, the home should be a place of fun and laughter. There is nothing quite as sad as a home hungry for humor, a family failing at fun, or a marriage minus mirth. And yet, many families are in just such a depressing state. They take themselves too seriously. They view relationships as a burden to endure, rather than a blessing to enjoy. Into the ears of such I have to scream: Lighten up!

A child should see his family unit as being a place where sincere, authentic fun is generated. Family time too often teeters on the edge of boring. I want my kids to see me as godly. I want them to see me as an intelligent thinker and problem solver. I want them to see me as a lover of their mother and a good provider. But I also want them to see me as a suitor and wooer of fun.

WHAT FUN IS

When I say "fun," I don't mean frivolous or foolish, what my grandmother would call "tom-foolery." I mean using the light touch in what we say and how we act, and including fun activities at home, even games like hide-and-seek. We can't take something so infinitely important as family life and wrap it in boredom. I've learned that no matter what a family does together, it can be peppered with pleasure.

Mowing and edging a lawn is not what I call having fun. I don't look forward to it. I don't get that feeling of excitement in the pit of my stomach when I drive by the house and see the grass too high. I don't get that "can't wait" attitude, and neither did my son. When I would tell him on Friday afternoon that the yard needed some attention from us on Saturday, he would always conjure up that excited facial look and say, "Oh, please Dad, can I do it?" (Our little joker made his point cleverly.) Yet after a couple hours of sweat and drudgery (by the way, we always did a bang-up job), we would sort of hang out together, surveying our handiwork with a cold drink in our hand, and truthfully enjoy even our toil together.

The way we kept our family unit on the edge of enjoyment was that we never took ourselves too seriously. We didn't allow the children to trample on the sacred or have "fun" at someone's expense, but most activity was open season for a clever pun or tasteful practical joke.

One form of harmless fun (providing everyone is comfortable with such teasing) is the practical joke. Members of many families like surprising one another with such jokes. In the Ledbetter household parents and children have developed the fine art of the practical joke. For instance, both my son and I play the trumpet. Motivated by the sincere desire to share our combined musical talents, we periodically gave others a demonstration of our blowing capacity—whenever the other had overslept. A perfectly peaceful state of early morning slumber came to an abrupt ending thanks to our gift of music. Needless to say, my son and I had several good laughs, and several life threats!

When Leah, my youngest daughter, was about seven years old, she desperately wanted a Nintendo game. We were unable to afford it ourselves, so my brother decided to give her one as a Christmas gift. It came in a rather large box. He placed it unwrapped under the tree. When Leah saw that box, she lost control of herself. She ran all over the house, jumping up and down while screaming "Yes! Yes! Yes!" Needless to say, she was excited.

While she wasn't paying attention, Leah's brother and sister decided to play a little trick on her. They took the box into another room, removed the game, refilled it with clothes, and placed it back under the tree. When the time came to open presents, everyone encouraged Leah to open the Nintendo box. She gladly complied. I'll never forget the look on her face, trying to portray gratitude for the clothes her uncle supposedly gave, while feeling great disappointment. The group broke out in laughter and let her in on the gag. Then they brought out the game, much to her relief. We still laugh together whenever we watch that family memory on videotape.

It was during such times of joy and laughter that our parent-child conversational and generational barriers came down. Of course, dear old Dad was a favorite target. And loved it. Heavy-handed authoritarian parenting will effectively crush true enjoyment. Joy and laughter, in contrast, will draw a family together.

It's fun to know and be a part of families that can laugh together. That's one reason two of the most popular television programs have been "The Cosby Show" and "Home Improvement." They feature families who, despite hardships, can enjoy the fun of just belonging to each other.

An important practical tip is necessary here. Parents, plan ahead so that nothing will put you into a grumpy, complaining "wet blanket" mood. The children will do their level best, perhaps in ignorance or perhaps on purpose, to raze the best of recreational plans you can make. Don't allow it—after all, isn't that why we call them children?

MAKING THE CHOICE TO ENJOY LIFE

I'm not suggesting that you make every area of life a foolish frolic in the sun. What I am saying is that life here is way too short to always wear a long face. Even the areas of life we could count as grinding, we can choose to see as enjoyment, because they comprise but one aspect of our lives, and an aspect over which we have no control. Therefore we can choose not to let that area overwhelm or depress us. Instead, let's recognize life as always moving forward, offering new experiences. Otherwise, by concentrating on the ills of the moment, we just might miss the promise of the future.

Paint on the canvas of your mind a family where joy and laughter are as common as eating and sleeping, a place where recreation creates that pocket of freedom for children to flourish, where parents can model in deed what cannot be taught in word.

FRAGRANCE FIVE: AFFIRMATION

How can parents help build an identity for their child? How can a support system be put into place? It begins with affirmation and praise, both forms of encouragement. Mom and Dad must fill the dual role of head cheerleaders when it comes to their kids. Constantly affirm the fact that the circumstances are only temporary hoops through which the child must jump. Encourage him or her to keep moving forward in all areas of life and not give up. A child who is affirmed at home will become an adult who can take on the world!

STATEMENTS OF AFFIRMATION

Here are just a few statements that can affirm your children:

"You can be anything you want to be."
"I know you'll give it your best!"
"Chin up! You gave it a great effort."
"I'm proud of you."
"You're still first string on my team."
"I trust you."

These are statements our kids need to hear from us. They are part of affirming their worth, building their confidence, and creating a sweet-smelling family fragrance.

AFFIRMATION FOR A TRUMPET PLAYER

Affirmation is crucial, both from parents and others whom your children respect. When I entered junior high school, I enrolled in band. I was confident I could make it as a trumpeter, for I had played piano from age six. Indeed, I became proficient, soon winning the first (lead) chair and holding that position through most of my secondary school life.

My friend Johnny seemed to constantly challenge my position. He was a good trumpet player too, and he wanted first chair. A rule had been set by our band director that every two months the first chair could be challenged. So I was forever defending my status.

During my senior year in high school, the day for the challenge came around about the same time I had a mouth sore on my top lip. I'm not much of a whiner, so I showed up for the challenge. I didn't do well, and I lost my chair. Later that week, someone mentioned to the director about the canker on my lip. The director, Mr. Sonnenburg, called me into the band office to ask if it was true.

"Yes," I answered, pulling my lip up to reveal the sore. Mr. Sonnenburg immediately negated the results, and he restored me to the position of first chair. He rescheduled the challenge, and two weeks later, I held off Johnny's challenge and remained the first-chair trumpet player.

Mr. Sonnenburg affirmed me that day, and I developed an appreciation and respect for my band director. It may seem a small thing to some, but to this teenage boy it taught a memorable lesson: Words and actions of trust and loyalty can give us confidence; and in return we often show loyalty to those who affirm us.

DECLARE, DON'T DENY

There's a second lesson from my trumpet challenge and my director's affirmation. When a child's confidence is shaken and his or her "position" is challenged, he needs affirmation. Often the feeling of being worthless seizes a child in its grip and creates an identity crisis. Circumstance begins its dictatorial reign. That's when a parent should reassure the child of his unchanging position in the family. This is not the time to equivocate or make a degrading remark about the performance. Instead, declare with enthusiasm his identity and position in your heart.

Deny a child affirmation and he will grow up incessantly seeking it. Success in the business world or any other pursuit will sit second chair to your child's insatiable desire for approval. He or she will move from job to job, from friend to friend, from activity to activity, seeking to fill the void left over from childhood.

A child whose position is constantly affirmed will overcome temporal setbacks and adverse circumstances and be firmly rooted, enabling him to withstand outside challenges. That kind of affirmation should not come solely from teachers, ministers, counselors, or other friends. It should come from the place designed to give it: the family.

Another key to affirming your kids is being enthusiastic, rather than apathetic, when it comes to the things they are involved with. We need to be engaged with their accomplishments and interests. We need to care about the things they care about. When they carry home an indiscernible finger painting from preschool, they need us to hang it on the refrigerator door to show our excitement. When they achieve a good grade on a school paper, they need us to read the paper with a sense of anticipation. When they get cut from the varsity squad, they need us to call the coach a jerk! Not really. But they do need a supportive arm around a sagging shoulder, letting them know we care about the things that affect their lives.

Enthusiastic families are busy families. It is hard work going to all the games, helping with the homework, driving for the field trips, hosting the banquets, shopping for that new dress, and attending every performance of the school play featuring Junior in a minor part. It isn't easy staying engaged with the things every child does. But few things yield more rewards or communicate more love to our kids.

GETTING PERSONAL

Understanding the need for a loving, supporting "family fragrance" is one thing. Doing something to create it is another. The following questions may help you get started. Take a few moments to evaluate your efforts to date in creating an environment of love.

1. How effective have you been at the process of creating a sweet-smelling aroma in your home by practicing The Fragrance Five? Identify your areas of strength and weakness. Grade your home from one to five, circling the appropriate number. Use the following scale:

> 1 = not at all
> 2 = rarely
> 3 = sometimes
> 4 = often
> 5 = always

Affection—

Is love demonstrated and expressed frequently in your home?

1   2   3   4   5

Respect—

Are family members treated with the respect they deserve?

1   2   3   4   5

Order—

Are there clearly defined rules, roles, and rights in your family?

1   2   3   4   5

Merriment—

Does your family laugh and have fun together?

1   2   3   4   5

Affirmation—

Are accomplishments praised and celebrated?

1   2   3   4   5

2. Identify one thing you can do in the next week to improve your family fragrance in each of the five areas.

Affection—

In order to demonstrate my love I will . . .

_____

_____

_____

Respect—

In order to guarantee others are treated with respect I will . . .

_____

_____

_____

Order—

In order to establish a sense of order in my home I will . . .

_____

_____

_____

Merriment—

In order to foster fun as a family together I will . . .

_____

_____

_____

Affirmation—

In order to affirm and praise others, I will . . .

_____

_____

_____

Congratulations! You've taken one small step toward creating an environment of love. Keep it up. Before you know it, your family fragrance will be sweeter than you ever thought possible.

Chapter Eight

IMPRESSION POINTS

J im and Janet watch their three children decorate the plastic-covered table. In drips and drabs, the toothpaste spreads across the tabletop; the three young kids are having the time of their lives squeezing the paste out of the tube. Jim watches closely, a smile ever-present. It's all part of his plan.

"OK," Dad says, slapping a twenty-dollar bill onto the table. "The first person to get the toothpaste back into their tube gets this money!" Little hands begin working to shove the peppermint pile back into rolled-up tubes. They have very little success, of course. "We can't do it, Dad!" protests the youngest child.

"The Bible tells us that's just like your tongue," Dad answers. "Once the words come out, it's impossible to get them back in. So be careful what you say because you may wish you could take it back." The children look at Dad and each other and smile. An unforgettable impression is made.

Most weeks Jim and his wife succeed in creating "impression points" for their kids. It's a weekly routine in the Wiedmann home, adopted several years ago, when Jim, talking to a neighbor family learned about the strategy for teaching children valuable truths. One night each week, those neighbors spent time intentionally "impressing" their kids with their values and beliefs through a weekly ritual called "Family Night." They play games, talk, study, and do the things which reinforce the importance of family and faith.

Jim decided to bring this concept into his own home— and launched his own "Family Night" routine. It is during these times that he intentionally creates impression points with his kids. The impact? His kids are able to repeat, and more importantly model, the lessons they've learned over the past few years. It makes Dad proud, as well it should. He is putting forth the effort, and a heritage is being passed.

Not all impression points come by planning. As we will see, some of the best occur when our children do something unexpected and we respond. Such events are teachable moments when we can impress our kids with deeper truth. For instance, had Jim stumbled on the children smearing the toothpaste without his permission, he had a teachable moment in the offing. He could then yell at them, or he could use their mess as an object lesson—to create an impression point.

WHAT ARE IMPRESSION POINTS?

Impression points are a valuable tool in your heritage chest, and they are easy to access, for we make impressions every day of our lives. We impress upon others our values, preferences, and concerns. We do it through our talk and our actions. We do it intentionally, and we do it incidentally.

Sometimes we turn our children on to our ideas. Other times we turn them off. Parents who are able to make impression points work for them, rather than against them, have mastered a very powerful art: how to inscribe upon their children's heart truths contained in events in their lives.

What are impression points? In short, impression points are those times in life when we make an impression upon others—when we "impress" them with who we are, what we think, or what we do. The impressions may come to our children through our words, but impression points contain more power and lasting effect when they come through instructive events our children can observe. Impression points can be intentionally created, or they can incidentally occur. Either way, they make an impression . . . for good or bad.

BACK IN TIME

Impression points have been used throughout history by many parents. Even God has used—and continues to use—impression points to instruct those for whom He cares. When the Jewish people had escaped Pharaoh's rule and stood at the edge of the Promised Land, God, who was ready to pour the sweetness of possessions into their lives, had a final debriefing session with Moses, the leader of the people.

Moses relayed God's instructions on how they could cope with the success that was awaiting. Significantly, Moses' words included a command to make lasting impressions on their children (Deuteronomy 6:5–7):

Love the Lord your God with all your heart and with all your soul and with all your strength. These commandments that I give you today are to be upon your hearts. Impress them on your children.

How were these Jewish parents to impress the commandments for a God-honoring life upon their children? According to Moses, they should

Talk about them when you sit at home and when you walk along the road, when you lie down and when you get up. Tie them as symbols on your hands and bind them on your foreheads. Write them on the doorframes of your houses and on your gates. (Deuteronomy 6:7–9)

God was on the verge of giving His people a large land with ready-made cities. He would provide houses filled with good things, water wells they wouldn't have to dig, crops they did not plant. He knew they would be filled to satisfaction. He also knew the dangers such satisfaction poses. When we become satisfied, our relationship with God seems to become less important, our relationship with the children suffers, and our diligence wanes. In addition, their possessions would consume their attention. Houses, wells, and farms would require constant care, endless improvements, and time-consuming upkeep. As they became very busy, they could neglect the process of teaching the next generation about what is truly important.

So, in order to keep them—and us—on track, God commanded His people to create and capitalize upon what we have labeled "Impression Points." The parents were instructed on how to use four distinct kinds of impression points.

FOUR KINDS OF IMPRESSION POINTS

Of course, when it comes to our children, the goal is to make a positive impression. We seek to give them a solid spiritual, emotional, and social legacy. The four broad categories identified in Deuteronomy 6:5–9 can help us wield the powerful tool of impression points. The four kinds are: verbal impression points, symbolic impression points, visual impression points, and journalized impression points.

VERBAL IMPRESSION POINTS

As parents, we must talk about our values all day, every day, repeatedly. Our speech should reflect what really matters. As the Lord said through Moses, "Talk about them when you sit at home, when you walk along the road, when you go to bed, and when you get up in the morning."

In the Ledbetter family, that point of connection always has been around the dinner meal. My wife would set the table every evening at 5:30 with china, silver, and candle-light, even though some meals were as simple as her scrumptious potato soup and a salad. It was at those meals that we subtly instructed our children.

Here, too, we engaged our children in open communication. At the dinner table principle could be questioned with impunity, and we tried to give sincere answers. The conversations ranged from the simple to the complex. Sometimes a certain subject could be our topic on several occasions before coming to a suitable solution.

When Becky was almost five, she began to stutter out a sentence during one dinner. "Dad," she asked, looking at me with her head tilted to the left and her big dark brown eyes flashing, "what's a b--?" I must admit, she caught us off guard with that vulgar word. I almost fell off my chair laughing at her childish innocence; yet we had to respond to that profane word for an immoral woman. My wife, who always stays calm and makes up for my "falling over stunned laughter," gently retorted, "Where did you hear that word, Becky?"

Gail then engaged Becky in an extended conversation. She found pertinent information, explained the idea behind the word, and then countered the word. We never heard of it again. It was a teachable moment, and rather than merely rebuking Becky, Gail was able to turn the word into a verbal impression point.

Another verbal impression point occurred during our trip to Disneyland several years ago. Disneyland is only a half-day's drive (six hours) from our house, and we decided to spend a couple of days as a family in Southern California, including a grand visit to the home of Mickey and Donald. We love the Pacific coastline, and Disneyland had several new shows, so we knew the mini-vacation was a winner. We were going to be in the car several hours with our children, a perfect time to relax—and to impress values on our children.

A few miles out of town Gail and I began to talk about some of our dating experiences, and the children listened eagerly. Matthew, thirteen, and Becky, twelve, were amused to think that we actually ever dated. After Gail and I laughed together and were laughed at by our junior highers, my wife said, "I brought this tape about sexual bonding. Let's hear what it has to say." Intentionally, we listened to the tape.

The message yielded some brisk conversation afterward. But more than the conversation, it made a compelling impression on Matt and Becky that would influence their future relationships. Right there in the car some resolve was inculcated into their virtues. We enjoyed Disneyland, but a longer-lasting benefit of the trip was the open discussion about sex with our two older children.

Verbal impression points can occur anywhere—on the road, on the beach, in the bedroom. But the most common place for you probably can be around the kitchen table, during or after a meal. Each weeknight at the dinner table affords ample opportunity for verbalizing. Mothers have special opportunities with younger children reading in bed with them. (Dads, of course, can do this equally well.) Fairy tales often contain moral lessons, and children's Bible stories offer many truths about God and our own selfish natures. We can read the stories and discuss them. During such quiet moments with our children, we often, unaware, pass our values and at the same time draw closer to our children. This is how we impress our kids with who we are, and convey to them important truths.

Parents, take opportunities with your children to verbalize. Talk about the things that are important—when you sit at home, when you walk along the road, when you go to bed, and when you get up in the morning.

SYMBOLIC IMPRESSION POINTS

The second kind of impression point is described in Deuteronomy 6:8: "Tie them as symbols on your hands."

Symbolism is a powerful way to impress your values upon your children. Some parents still use a symbolic device to help their memories: They tie a string around their index finger. The string is representative of what they need to remember. If the rent is due, the string symbolizes the rent payment. If a birthday or anniversary is upcoming, the string symbolizes a gift that should be purchased.

Why a string? Why not place the rent check in your purse or coat pocket where you will see it, or a calendar there, with the anniversary date circled? You could do that, of course, but the string is an unusual reminder, a picture that reminds you that something special must be done this day. Symbols are special, pictorial reminders of what we must do or something we believe in.

We wear symbols all the time. Our jacket with the logo of our favorite sports team symbolizes where our loyalty lies. Teens wear clothing with designer tags that symbolize a social status. Gangs have wardrobe, signals, and colors that symbolize their intentions. Symbols are all around.

We, as parents, cannot escape symbolism. Our lives symbolize our values. Our actions and our lifestyle form the string around the proverbial finger, reminding our children of what is important.

We sang a song in Sunday school when I was a child that went like this:

> Oh, be careful little eyes what you see . . .
> Oh, be careful little ears what you hear . . .
> Oh, be careful little hands what you do . . .
> And be careful little feet where you go . . .

The song taught us that what our faculties participated in was symbolic of the condition of our heart. Children are neither blind nor ignorant. They pick up quickly that the things we do represent who we really are and what we secretly believe. Thus our faculties can symbolize our desire for wealth, power, or fame. Or they can symbolize to our children our compassion or our desire to give.

Kids pick up on symbols. That is why God told Moses to instruct the parents to impress valuable symbols on their children. Our words symbolize to our children our values. What we extol dictates our stroll.

But what we don't say also can speak as loud as what we say. In our home, Gail and I never resorted to name-calling. Our heated exchanges were private. How we spoke to each other was guarded, because it all symbolized our true relationship. We did not announce our disagreements in front of our kids. Nor did we criticize or question others in front of them. If they heard us discussing someone, it would amount to gossip. The quickest path to bring children to an embittered spirit is to condemn others in front of them. It is symbolic of your inner feelings.

How can you symbolize respect, kindness, and compassion to your children? Here are just a few ways. Always back their teachers or other authorities over their petty battles. That symbolizes how you feel about response to authority. Attend church regularly and give to ministry. That symbolizes how you love God. Touch your spouse in front of your children. A kiss, an embrace in the home or out in public is a powerful symbol of your love, and it symbolizes security for them. We were modest. Do not appear nude or immodestly dressed; being fully clothed symbolizes the worth of a person's privacy.

In all these ways, we "tie them as symbols" around the fingers of our sons and daughters, giving them important reminders and examples of what counts in life.

VISUAL IMPRESSION POINTS

We discover a third kind of impression point in Moses' command to "hang them in front of your eyes." Eventually many Jewish readers would literally hang a small box on their forehead containing a scriptural message. Today, we can offer our children a visual demonstration of biblical principles.

Consider this. A child will remember 10 percent of what he or she hears, but 50 percent of what he sees. Thus, what our children see at home is far more powerful than what they hear.

Here are two types of visual impressions you can make. First, help your kids "envision" right decisions before they're confronted with choices. Gail and I, for instance, created what-if stories where a decision had to be made, and helped them envision the solution. For instance, if they were staying at a friend's house and someone suggested watching a sexually explicit movie on TV, what would be the proper response? We painted the scenario ahead of time and formed the solution. We taught our kids how to avoid being placed in compromising positions by deciding ahead of time not to make a hasty decision after the back windows of the car were steamed over with passion. At that point it's too late.

Second, "hang in front of your eyes" pictures and words that reinforce the values you seek to instill. Picture books, artwork, and house decorations all can do that. When our children were still very young, Gail bought books that had beautifully created paintings or photographs. As they got older, classics replaced picture books. Help your children develop a love for reading, and you are giving them a powerful way to learn values (as they learn to discern, with your help, quality stories and pictures). Reading stimulates their imagination in the right direction through the words and objects on a page.

How about the decorations of your home? Kurt still recalls the saying on one of the decorative wall hangings in his home, which made a daily impression just hanging there:

"Big people talk about ideas.
Average people talk about things.
Small people talk about other people."

Elsewhere in the house, Kurt glanced at a painting of an old man giving thanks before eating a small bowl of soup and lump of bread. The humble man with the wrinkled and meager rations became a routine reminder that Kurt had much for which to be thankful. In front of the kitchen sink hung Scripture verses. There his mother would spend time memorizing while cleaning pots and pans. All of those images served to reinforce the beliefs and values of Kurt's heritage.

Of course, the most powerful visual images that impact our children are our daily behaviors and choices. What they see us do has far more influence than what they hear us say.

Do they see us treating our husband or wife with respect and dignity at home?

Do they see us calling in sick to work just because we want a break?

Do they see us talk negatively about others behind their backs?

Do they see us forgiving others, or holding a grudge?

Do they see patience, or a quick temper?

Do they see personal discipline, or self-gratification?

Do they see us "cheat the system" now and then—at tax time, or when paying admission for a five year old at an "ages four and under free" park? (Ouch!)

Remember, the little things we do day in and day out serve as visual impression points. Make them what they should be. "Fifty percent of what they can see" is a lot of impressing.

WRITTEN IMPRESSION POINTS

The fourth impression point comes from writing: "Write them on the doorframes and on the gates." Whether you write them on the doorframe, the gates, or in a notebook, the things that are important to you should be recorded and later shared with your children.

Create a journal that has entries about events and your responses that indicate your values. The entries can include lists of things you know contribute to successful living, as well as lists of things to avoid.

King Solomon, called the wisest man who ever lived, (he asked and received from God great wisdom), chose to record his great insights on the human experience in a book. Proverbs probably was written to preserve his wisdom for future generations to glean. You might call most of the Old Testament book of Proverbs "Solomon's Log of Journalized Impression Points." And the subtitle could easily be "Listen, My Son." Significantly, this wise man chose to write to his son wise words about life.

The phrase "listen, my son" recurs in the book of Proverbs, as Solomon tries to impress upon his own children the things God had taught him about life and living. He shared how to handle money, business guidelines, the folly of wild living, the dangers of seductive women, the benefits of clean living, and, of course, the ultimate value of understanding. Solomon knew that the Lord, as the great architect of human affairs, could be trusted to outline the best plan for successful living. And so, he took the time to share that wisdom with his offspring. As a result, we all have the benefit of his timeless insight. He wrote it down!

Someday death will engulf us all. The written word can become an enduring means of impressing our thoughts and values upon the next generation.

After twenty-seven years, I still like to read on occasion the letters my girlfriend (now my wife) wrote me when we were courting. Her words are as fresh as the day they were written. They remind me of the things she liked in me, and some of the qualities I appreciate in Gail. All I have to do is open one, read the contents, and memories flood back into my mind.

We can give the same lasting records to our children. Whether it's bringing home report cards, getting their first coat and tie, having significant birthdays, marching in graduations, or achieving in sports or academics, events large and small are great opportunities for us to write to them. Our letters and journal entries will impress on them values as we brag to them about character they showed through their accomplishments. (Teach your children early to also journalize and remember their thoughts at these times.) Don't minimize the importance of writing things down. Almost all of us can recall books or articles we read at different points that gave us the precise answer at the correct moment. We found comfort because other people believed in journalizing their values. They believed in writing down solutions they had discovered. Without their commitment to writing it down, we the readers would be poorer.

I wish for myself as I grow older that my parents, grandparents, and great-grandparents had written their experiences down, and how their opinions, as to what life taught them, affected or changed their lives. Every once in a while, my dad or mother will verbalize things passed to them from their parents, and I become captivated. I wish I had access to my grandparents' experiences, thoughts, and teachings via the written page. Then, though dead, they could still speak with power and wisdom from their graves.

Kurt has a letter-writing plan I highly commend. Every year on their birthdays, Kurt writes each of his young boys a letter. He describes their personalities, the major events of the past twelve months, and describes how much he loves them and what things really matter in life. He is saving these letters to give his boys when they are older as a lasting legacy of their father's love. This "journalized" impression point is formal today, but will likely lead to many informal conversations in years to come that will give Kurt even more opportunity to impress his children's lives.

Parents, write it down! Someday, you'll be glad you did.

INTENTIONAL VS. INCIDENTAL IMPRESSION POINTS

The impression points listed in Deuteronomy are both intentional and incidental in nature. Intentional impression points are those we create; they are planned. Incidental impression points, on the other hand, just happen. They occur in the everyday of life, and they happen whether we are ready for them or not. They represent teachable moments that await our response, and we must be ready to take hold of such moments.

THE ROLE OF TRADITIONS AND CUSTOMS

As parents, you can begin early the process of intentionally impressing your values into the lives of your children. You'll be surprised how traditions, practices, and customs begun years ago will still be in place years later, bringing a special sense of community and anticipation to your family. And the process of creating intentional impression points will give birth to all sorts of wonderfully unexpected incidental impression points. In fact, quite often, the incidental you don't plan will be better and more effective than the intentional you had diligently prepared. But without the intentional effort, the incidental activities would not have materialized.

Of course, it goes both ways. There will be times when something unexpected happens, creating a wonderful opportunity to intentionally impress our values to the kids. The key, again, is recognizing such occasions and capitalizing on the moment. Leroy Dowell, a successful businessman in Hobbs, New Mexico, once hired his teenage daughter Lynn for the summer in hopes that he would have intentional impression points for her. He felt there would be many lessons for her: learning the value of diligent work, experiencing the surprises and disappointments of people in the workplace, seeing how people advance successfully, and gaining confidence as a person.

The greatest lesson Lynn learned, however, was not planned by her father. During the summer Leroy was falsely accused of unethical business practices. Being in the office, Lynn knew the charges were untrue. She watched how her dad handled the lies and the accusers scrupulously, with wisdom, justice, and charity. Leroy had wanted to teach his daughter what the workplace was like. But in that unexpected development, Lynn observed her father's moral and ethical standards and learned far more incidentally than she would have by her father's intentional plans.

WHEN THE INTENTIONAL
LEADS TO THE INCIDENTAL

The key word related to impression points is *creating*. Someone must take the time to purposefully plan the intentional. The incidental opportunities will come on occasion, but the planned opportunities can be more regular. (And, remember, they can lead to incidental impression points.)

I cherish the times when my boy and I could talk seriously about girls. More often than not, those conversations occurred as an incidental outgrowth of an intentional outing.

Several times Gail and I took the kids to formal restaurants to teach them etiquette. Often those formal occasions created informal impression points in very humorous and embarrassing ways. On one occasion, I invited a nationally known speaker to our church. He accepted, graciously adding us to his busy itinerary. We went to a local restaurant for lunch immediately after the service. My wife wanted to take Leah, then age ten, to create an impression point. All the way to the restaurant Gail instructed our little chatterer on etiquette. She told Leah not to talk because the guest was in a hurry, and Dad and he had some important business to discuss.

Leah did great! She listened quietly until near the end of lunch, but then she could hold out no longer. At a small break in the conversation, she jumped in and seriously asked, "Mr. Ragle, were some of those stories you told at church true, or were you just making a point?" The guest almost slid under the table laughing, while Mom and I stared at each other wide-eyed before busting up with laughter.

We used the incident later as a launching point to discuss the value of not saying everything you think.

I could list a thousand similar incidents. At such times intentional impression points cry out for creation!

EARNING THE RIGHT TO IMPRESS

The emotional development pattern of children only gives us a limited window of opportunity in which we can earn the right to impress. During these early years we must become a trusted friend and respected mentor if we hope to influence their lives as they mature. Follow four simple guidelines, and you will earn the right to impress.

1. BE THERE

Absent or detached parents don't impress. Frolic with your children while they are very young. At times it may seem like there are a thousand "more important" things to do. But it will pay tremendous dividends in the long run. Why? Because you are earning the right to impress. Teach them how to interact. Be an example in keeping your cool. Show them how important they are by spending precious time with them. Don't offer them your leftover, fatigued, half-interested time slots. Give them a piece of your quality time. It will speak volumes to them.

2. BE FAIR

Children have an innocent, straightforward desire to do what is fair and be treated fairly. Striving to be fair should not cause you to always have to sit down and ponder what to do. Being fair means you will be clear in your instructions. It means you will be open and honest with your feelings, being frank without being harsh. You will always be equitable. That means you will be equal in regards to the rights of each child.

3. BE CONSISTENT

Nothing will undermine your ability to impress faster than inconsistency. The Scriptures say it this way: "A double-minded man is unstable in all his ways . . . let your yea be yea; and your nay, nay" (James 1:8; 5:12, KJV). If something is bad for your children when you are euphoric, then it is also bad for them when you are depressed. We often allow our feelings to dictate our parenting skills. Our disposition determines our answers, forcing the kids to determine the bias of our mood before they ask important questions. Unwittingly, we force them to master the art of manipulation.

Remember, consistency is the mark of a follower of Christ. "Jesus Christ is the same yesterday and today and forever" (Hebrews 13:8).

If you are given to mood swings, deal with them so the kids don't have to. Don't allow how you feel to dictate how you parent.

4. BE PREDICTABLE

Martha attended one church where I was a pastor, yet I admit I tried to avoid her like the flu. In fact, I almost would rather catch the flu than encounter her. The flu only lasted a couple of days, after all. I have never met such an unpredictable person. One Sunday I might be smothered in honey, and the next, I might be spewed upon with hot breath.

Martha could swell up and explode one day, then the next show genuine humility. I don't think it was hypocrisy or schizophrenia, just unpredictable and unsettling changes in behavior. The only words my mind would say to me after an encounter with Martha would be "go figure."

Imagine what that's like to our children. Indeed, our kids sometimes find us as parents equally unpredictable. It shakes them. It makes us unapproachable. It pushes them away. Predictability helps give our children a balanced approach to life.

Be there, be fair, be consistent, be predictable. All these are a part of the prerequisite attitudes that help parents earn the latent license that allows them to impress their children.

LASTING IMPRESSIONS

When my son was in the seventh grade, he took an electronics course in school. In this class students learned sophisticated information about building electronic devices. Matt chose as his major project a computer monitor screen. He would build it from a kit purchased for that project. During the course of that semester, we continually encouraged him to do a good job, learn all the "how tos," and create a useful tool for someone's computer. The class sold the projects, then, as a fund-raiser. We intentionally bid on his project and secretly purchased it. Then we wrapped it up for Christmas along with the other components of a new computer. To his surprise, on Christmas morning he received the new computer he wanted for Christmas, along with his own monitor.

Besides our desire to encourage Matt, we purchased his monitor hoping to create an intentional impression point. It worked; we had a lively exchange about pride of workmanship and learning by doing. Matt agreed, from his experience, that a worker should always give his best, as if the item were going to be his own—because it just might be. We still have the monitor, and it still shows his careful workmanship.

GETTING PERSONAL

If capturing and creating "impression points" with our children is the key to influencing their lives, then we must take action now. For most parents, making an impression fails not because of missing desire but a missing plan. This "Getting Personal" will let you evaluate how well you have planned and how to start making plans.

1. How well have you done at creating intentional and recognizing incidental "impression points" with your family? Rate yourself in the following categories. Grade yourself from one to five for each, circling the appropriate number. Use the following scale:

1 = not at all
2 = rarely
3 = sometimes
4 = often
5 = always

Verbal Impressions—

How often do I talk to my children about important, lasting issues?

1   2   3   4   5

Symbolic Impressions—

How well does my behavior symbolize my values?

1   2   3   4   5

Visual Impressions—

Do I help my children visualize what is true and right?

1   2   3   4   5

Written Impressions—

Do I write down the things that are important for my children to understand?

1   2   3   4   5

2. Identify one thing you can do in the next week to create an impression point in each category.

Verbal—

In order to impress my children through conversation I will . . .

_____

_____

_____

Symbolic—
  In order to symbolically reinforce my values I will . . .

_____

_____

_____

Visual—
  In order to help my children visualize truth and right I will . . .

_____

_____

_____

Written—
  In order to record my values for my children I will . . .

_____

_____

_____

3. Identify two occasions in the past week when you missed an opportunity to capitalize upon an incidental impression point in your home.

  1. When _____ occurred, I should
           (Describe Incident)

     have _____ in order to
          (Describe Action)

     impress _____ upon my family.
             (Describe Value)

2. When _____ occurred, I should
              (Describe Incident)

   have _____ in order to
              (Describe Action)

   impress _____ upon my family.
              (Describe Value)

Those who walk through this little exercise on a regular basis will become more aware and disciplined in their efforts to impress their children.

Chapter Nine
THE RIGHT ANGLE

Ronnie burst into my office wide-eyed and half hysterical. I stood from behind my desk and walked around to greet him as he sucked air to keep from sobbing.

"Why don't you have a seat and let's talk about it, Ronnie," I said, trying to settle his emotions a little. I knew what I was dealing with, because Ronnie and I had had many conversations before, and this one was going to cover the exact same subject. I could easily become frustrated with him if I let myself.

Ronnie is forty and out of control; he's coming to talk about his thirteen year old son, Kevin, also out of control. That household has in it two junior highers emotionally, and the sad part is, the thirteen-year-old isn't nearly so much the problem as his father is. Ronnie was raised without what we have labeled a "right angle," and he is rearing his son in like manner. Growing up, Ronnie had no plumb line, or standard, to help him build his life straight and true. Now as an adult, Ronnie tries to raise his son correctly, but the harder he works, the more frustrated he becomes and the farther they both move away from the goal.

Wilber, a friend who sets tiles, once explained to me how he keeps all those tiny tiles in a straight line horizontally and vertically. After finding a level line near to the floor, he uses a piece of equipment called a ninety-degree angle. With this right angle he can draw a truly vertical plumb line on the wall; everything in that room is measured by its standard.

"One time I tried to eyeball it," he said with a grin. "All the way up the wall, it looked right to me until I was about two-thirds done. I stood back and was horrified. It was so far off. The more I worked up the wall, the farther off the angle I got. In the midst of the task, it didn't seem wrong. But it was, and it cost me a great deal. I had to re-do the entire job!"

I've experienced a similar frustration playing golf. When I tee off on a straight four-hundred-yard hole, and drive the ball only seventy-five yards, and am 15 percent off dead center, I will still be in the fairway and in pretty good shape. I still can see the green. But if I drive the ball two hundred seventy yards at 15 percent off center, I am way out of bounds and in big trouble. If, by some miracle, I am able to drive it four hundred yards at a 15 percent angle, I'm better than three hundred seventy-five feet to the right of the green. In anybody's game, that is bad golf.

Golf is just a game; life is not. That's why we need a right angle, a tool in our heritage chest that lets us draw an accurate vertical line to show our children what is right. The right angle will keep our children on track, showing them what is normal, healthy living. Just as a tiler can't set each tile on the wall at its own angle and expect the finished product to look as it should, our children cannot have a healthy, accurate perspective on life without a straight plumb, which comes by having a true right angle measure.

For a strong heritage, we define the right angle this way: *The right angle is the standard of normal, healthy living against which our children will be able to measure their attitudes, actions, and beliefs.*

RIGHT IN OUR OWN EYES

Ronnie was raising his child by "eyeballing"—taking an educated guess concerning—what he should do with his son. At one particular moment one thing seemed right, and at another moment something else seemed right. It wasn't until he was forced to stand back and take a good look that he realized he had perpetuated the wrong angle. Too late, he realized that his son was way off the mark from "normal." His hysteria came when he saw other children plumbed to the right angle and realized he could not move his own child's situation immediately back to the plumb line. Just like that tile setter, he worked long and hard . . . everything seemed right at the time. How could he be so far off now?

IF IT FEELS GOOD . . .

The Old Testament book called Judges contains an answer to Ronnie's perplexing situation. "When there was no king in Israel, everyone did that which was right in his own eyes." In the absence of a godly king, chaos ensued. Whatever suited the community at that moment was the definition of right. "If it feels good, do it!" became their motto. The people lived in total disregard of the right angle standard God had given.

As a result, the people lived way off center and raised their children off center. They worshipped heathen idols, and they forgot the God who had done so much for them. As it turns out, the Lord had to allow foreign powers to conquer and enslave His people in order to get their attention and get them back on track. Because they ignored the plumb line they were given, God had to step in and "redo the entire job."

It is much easier to do it right the first time. Many parents experience unnecessary frustration and heartache due to "eyeball" parenting. But the role of Mom or Dad is too important to be treated so lightly. The kids need us to take the task seriously. They need us to clearly establish "normal" in their lives. This means order and rules, of course, as discussed in chapter 7, but it also means setting standards based on God's rules.

During a course on counseling people with drug or alcohol addiction, I remember the teacher telling us, "One of the first things you must understand is adult children of alcoholics (ACA) do not know what normal is—so they perpetuate the abnormal."

I looked at my stack of handouts prepared for the class by the teacher, and there, second on the list of proper responses to ACA, were his words: "You must establish what normal should be in their lives. You can't get to normal if you don't know where or what it is."

His words are true. After working with many abusers and the abused, I have found their actions and thinking way off normal, way off the plumb line (right angle). Raised under abnormal values, they view their own experience as typical. Carrying this perception of normal into adulthood, they often raise their own children by the same standard.

SEEING CLEARLY

I began wearing a pair of eyeglasses in the tenth grade, after a teacher observed me squinting to see the chalkboard and told my parents. Eventually an ophthalmologist examined me and gave my parents a prescription for eyeglasses. I will never forget the day we went to pick them up. After I put them on, I saw things I had never seen before. The asphalt had small black rocks mixed together in it. The street signs were easily visible, and the chalkboard was incredibly clear.

Honestly, before I wore glasses, I thought everyone saw as I did. I thought everyone had to squint. I thought everyone had trouble reading street signs and chalkboards. To me, the abnormal I was subjected to was normal, until my vision was corrected. I began to live by a different standard of normal. Even today, I have a periodic eye exam to make sure I maintain the healthy perception I was given with my first pair of glasses.

CHECKPOINTS FOR HEALTHY PARENTING

There are several "checkpoints" you will need as you rear your children along the right angle to establish and maintain "normal" in all areas of their lives. Though by no means comprehensive, these items provide us with a starting place as we seek to avoid the error of "eyeball" parenting. It is at home that the right angle must be clearly set for each, lest outside influences be allowed to set the norm, some of which may be way off center.

1. SELF-WORTH

Experts tell us that a child knows by the time he/she is only a few weeks old whether he is wanted. Though an infant cannot speak, he or she can receive your communication. The tone of your voice, the way in which the child is handled, the routine of his feeding habits, the noise or chaos in the home, the time spent together, the early, loving discipline, and the relationships between family members are all significant means of communicating to the youngest child the status of his/her self-worth. He can begin to almost instinctively understand whether he is a pleasure or a nuisance.

Within the first year of life, the fragile worth of a child can be either established or seriously damaged. Nothing supersedes the value of positive affirmation at this point.

In one church where I was the pastor, I remember Beth, a little girl who had become as pushed down as her mother. The mother was overly submissive and happened to be crippled from an accident early in her life. The father had been accused of molesting a foster child in the home. From her parents, Beth had learned few personal hygiene or interpersonal skills. When I would see her at Sunday school, she was not too attractive with her unkempt hair and shyness that bordered on fear.

Beth hit a soft spot in my heart, and I determined that I would speak to her every time I saw her. I would invest in her self-worth, if I could. She became my project. Every

Sunday I would intentionally pass her class. Every Sunday and Wednesday evening I would look her up. "Hello, Sweetie," I would say. "Let me see your eyes . . . oh, I see real beauty inside you . . ." or "I love the color of your hair." Once I told her, "Your smile makes my heart sing." Each time I tried to point out an area of worth to her. It wasn't long before it became unnecessary for me to seek out little Beth . . . she found me.

For eight years, I kept this project going. Beth began to wash, to comb and brush her hair. She wanted to dress as nicely as she could for church, even if it was the same dress every week. Her eyes became unhooded and took on a sparkle. She smiled, even though her teeth weren't very straight. The night I saw her playing her flute in the church orchestra, a real joy washed over me.

Even today, when I visit that church, she smiles and greets me. She doesn't know to this day that she was my project. A little worth made her come alive. It will energize any child. It is a major checkpoint along the entire life of your child.

Closely aligned with self-worth is personal identity. If you have six children, none is the same as another. Each has his own personality. Each has his own talents and gifts. Each has his own personal growth pattern and direction. To treat a child as a mirror of another is to execute his identity. "Why can't you be what your brother was" or "You certainly aren't filling your sister's shoes" are mutilating maxims. Instead we must allow each child to be distinct. Learn his or her personality type, and let each child's identity survive intact as they enter adulthood.

Self-worth and identity checkpoints are vital. Keep them at the right angle.

2. PERSONAL RESPONSIBILITY

"Let him alone!" His voice was loud and firm. "Get away from him. Let him do it himself!" My eyes soon focused on a young boy who was big for his age. He had accidentally overturned a wheelbarrow full of dirt. The sheer weight of it falling to his left had thrown him to the ground. Several of the men helping at the construction site scurried over to help upright the wheelbarrow and re-fill it, when from across the yard his dad hollered those words.

The young boy dusted himself off, set the machinery upright, and began shoveling the dirt back into the wheel-barrow, glancing back toward his dad several times for some kind of approval. His dad quietly said to me, "He needs to learn responsibility. He needs to accomplish this job alone. He wanted to work, so let him work."

I understood the heart of that father. The boy finished his job and came back to his dad with a big grin; Dad greeted him by tousling his hair and saying, "Good job, son, you stayed with it." A seemingly minuscule interac-tion, but it had lifelong consequences. I witnessed a father mentoring his son in the area of responsibility.

By his actions in making his boy finish the task without help, Dad was saying, If you start a job, stay with it until it is complete. Don't make a mess and expect someone else to clean it for you. That was another brick mortared into the wall of his son's character.

When a child is given some responsibility around the house, it teaches him or her that there is a spot in the fam-ily where he or she fits. It teaches your child that if his responsibilities aren't upheld, the entire family unit is af-fected. Responsibility or irresponsibility will come with consequences, which will either help or hurt close rela-tionships. When Dad is negligent, or when Mom throws up her hands and walks out, the whole family ails.

Responsibility can and must be learned early on in the life of a child, so conscience and character become en-trenched enough that he/she will not permit the entire family unit to be affected. It is those three elements—con-science, consequence, and character—that work together to help lead us to goodness.

There are countless ways to reinforce responsibility in our children. And we must do that, for people naturally lean toward irresponsibility, so our children will want to avoid responsibility; they will want to neglect it and may even despise it. But they must learn it nonetheless. We must intentionally counter the inbred tendency toward laziness and negligence.

Here are three simple ways to teach your child to be responsible. *First, model responsibility.* Don't call in to the workplace sick if you aren't. Little ears are listening. Don't start a project and leave it unfinished. Little eyes are watching. *Second, teach it.* Tell your child why it is important to take responsibility seriously. Discuss the consequences of laziness. Instill an appreciation for the work ethic. *Third, give it.* The best way for a child to learn the discipline of responsibility is to be placed in a responsible position. Chores, caring for pets, and completing paper routes are just three ways a child learns to be responsible. Find something for your child to own, and hold him or her to it. Give responsibility.

Teaching responsibility has a side benefit: it helps your child learn to develop a work ethic that will serve him well as an adult. Doing chores inside the house or being responsible for a well-kept lawn teaches a child that others are counting on him to do a good job and that his skills fit a special niche that help others. He learns a sense of value in doing a task well.

3. DELAYED GRATIFICATION

Instant self-gratification has become the standard for this generation. From one-hour photo developing and instant oatmeal to almost-instant loan approval (thanks to computers), people want and often get their desires met quickly and fully. Your son and daughter can grow up thinking they too deserve to have it, and have it now.

But self-gratification is not a friend; he's an enemy. In fact, he's the death of dreams, for self-gratification cannot coexist with aspirations. He says, "Time is of the essence," yet knows not what essence really means. He only understands "yes" and never tolerates "no." He would have your children think there is no tomorrow, that if they pass anything up now, it may never come around again. He awakens their sleeping passions. He fills the present with sensations that serve to dull the sensibility of their future. The only way to contest him is to delay him. When delayed, he becomes innocuous, and your children have a chance at safety.

A child must learn early to replace the "normal" of instant gratification with the "healthy" of delayed gratification. Those who never learn to postpone never learn to prosper. And as author M. Scott Peck put it, parents have much to do with how well children learn the skill:

> For children to develop the capacity to delay gratification, it is necessary for them to have self-disciplined role models, a sense of self-worth, and a degree of trust in the safety of their existence. These "possessions" are ideally acquired through the self-discipline and consistent, genuine caring of their parents; they are the most precious gifts of themselves that mothers and fathers can bequeath.[1]

I once discussed this yearning to have things on a local radio program, "Family Matters." One morning during this daily call-in program, a young mother asked a very practical question: "How can we delay gratification, for instance, when wheeling up to the checkout stand at the grocery store? The store knows we have to stand in line. So they display all those goodies right there in front of the child."

We came to the conclusion that, if prepared in advance, she could bring a toy from home to distract the child just as her daughter reaches the checkout stand. Or she could carefully position herself between the child and the display, again, to distract the child. Distraction is the key in such situations, rather than being overly negative or, worse yet, caving in to the pressure by buying what he or she doesn't need to have.

Because young children have a very short attention span, distraction is our best weapon. But for an older child, reasoning the situation out beforehand is the key. "Now, Johnny, we aren't going to have a candy bar today because we're going to have ice cream after dinner. So don't even ask me when you see those candy bars at the store. Understand?" Advance discussion helps diffuse the inevitable encounter. Remember, it is important to use such occasions as opportunities to model the value of delayed gratification for your children.

When children always get what they want, they learn patterns that eventually lead to a fall and develop the desire for more, which is greed. A well-placed delay once in a while, even if what the child wants is not actually harmful, is an effective teacher. Notice I said "delay," not "omit." This principle works both ways. We should not deny our kids what they have earned, but they should earn it first. We all appreciate what cost us something— and that we waited for.

Of course, delayed gratification hinges on personal discipline. I believe personal discipline (health care, hygiene) is the precursor to a discipline in all other areas of a child's life. A look at how someone cares for his shoes can tell you a lot about the person. If we are lax in the small areas of life, we will probably be lax in larger areas also. Personal discipline helps self-worth. Care for this physical body means you care about your person. Helping your child with his self-esteem can begin by insisting on personal discipline. Such areas as a clean body, a clean room, a good feeling about oneself, and an ordered life often begin with a little bit of personal discipline.

4. SPIRITUAL EXPLORATION

For every child will come that time when he or she begins to probe for answers to spiritual questions. When a child begins to wonder about his spiritual being, he is giving you a natural opportunity to discuss standards, for he is considering his Creator to whom he is accountable. As parents, we must respond as our child's spiritual awareness blooms.

Earlier, we quoted Solomon where he said God had "set eternity in the hearts of men" (Ecclesiastes 3:11). With their innocence, children can sense spiritual realities early, and they will ask about them. We must be prepared, both to influence their eternal destiny and to help them see that standards come from God. I know several couples who have been forced to church by questions they could not answer.

Each of the following questions represents an opportunity to talk about spiritual truths and lasting standards. How many have you heard your child ask?

"Who made God?"

"Where does God live?"

"Is He small? He must be if He can live in my heart."

"Why do people die?"

"What is hell?"

"Where is heaven . . . where is hell?"

"Why did Grandpa die?"

And we should embrace teaching moments, for children are impressionable. I was driving a young boy home from Sunday school one day. His parents didn't attend church, and this was his first Sunday. On the way home we passed a long-haired, bearded fellow on a motorcycle, and the boy shouted, "Hey! There went Moses!" I couldn't convince him otherwise, either, because he had seen a bearded Moses on his teacher's flannel board.

Children are curious and are serious when they ask questions. When you begin to help them spiritually when they are young, and you establish spiritual checkpoints along their path, their spiritual thirst can be intensified. Let them ask the tough questions. Even if you don't feel confident to provide good answers, the process of inquiry should be encouraged, not avoided.

5. PRIORITIES

We live in an ordered universe, where plants and animals live a predictable existence and give sustenance, beauty, and pleasure to people. Humans, however, have a choice: they can give to others, or they can take. In His book of instructions, the Bible, God teaches us to give, and He helps with setting proper priorities.

Most of us usually take. Our children, like us, began that way, quickly choosing to take rather than give. And they usually choose the easy over the difficult: sweets over vegetables, play over learning, recess over the arithmetic book. Interestingly, God has put adults—themselves selfish and prone to take—in charge of children. As parents, we receive the demanding, yet exciting, challenge of forming and ordering the priorities of our young children. When we succeed, it's gratifying; when we don't, it's depressing.

In our family, Gail and I didn't view priorities as an exacting science. We didn't make lists. We lived by our priorities, and the children followed suit. When we observed them struggling with a priority, we came alongside and helped, reminding the kids of the importance of choosing based on what they held as important. When we witnessed them hanging with wrong friends, we counseled them through it. When it was bad music, we gave reasons why we disapproved and why they should not listen.

At one point, my son was interested in a girl we disapproved of very much because she was having a negative influence in his life, causing him to forget his priorities and convictions. When things began to go wrong in the relationship, I went to his room one evening. We talked, we prayed, and I gave him two weeks to break it off. "If you can't," I said, "I will."

He couldn't, so I did. Later he thanked me. "Dad," he said, "she had some kind of hold on me. I was powerless . . . thanks, Dad. I know it was the right thing."

Matthew didn't rebel, I believe, because we had started on priorities from an early age. Parents who are involved in helping their children set priorities are not being domineering; they are showing they care and are interested in their child's future. My son trusted my judgment, which was a crucial element in the order of his priorities. This and other incidents were opportunities for us to help Matthew establish and reinforce his life priorities. We did not point him to a list but rather came alongside as he worked through a tough life issue.

There are countless areas of life in which our kids need similar help setting proper priorities. They need to know that homework and piano practice comes before television. They need to know that television should be limited in time and content. (By the way, they need to know why, not just what programs they can watch.)

They also need to learn how to negotiate a balance between two seemingly important activities. Will family time always lose out to time with "the gang"? Is insisting on no Sunday shifts worth the risk of losing that fast-food job? Are getting the chores done vital when it means they may not complete a school assignment on time? And why was the assignment put off until the last minute? These and other issues need parental "coaching" if we expect them to master the art of setting proper life priorities.

6. SEXUALITY

The home is where human sexuality must be both affirmed and channeled. Some parents try to shame a child for the sexual interest he may feel. But that is wrong. Others exploit it. That is worse. Our job as parents is to model a healthy sexual life in the context of lifelong commitment, and to talk about sex as God's wedding gift to His children. Human sexuality is both wonderful and dangerous. Let's be sure to help our kids understand both aspects.

The right angle of a child's sexuality—the standard that sets a straight plumb line for a strong legacy socially, emotionally, and, yes, spiritually—is abstinence. Many adults think kids are going to experiment anyway. That's a flawed philosophy. Kids can be persuaded to delay sexual gratification.

The "True Love Waits" campaign (started by the Southern Baptist convention but now endorsed by many evangelical churches) is one of many teen-driven movements trying to bring respect back to the discipline of abstinence. Millions of young people are standing up and voicing their commitment to sexual purity at arenas, outdoor rallies, and at marches. They have signed pledges to remain virgins until marriage, despite enormous pressure from peers and the arts (especially the movies). In 1994, hundreds of thousands of these cards were brought to Washington, D.C., to reinforce a very important message: "Not everybody's doing it!"

Of course, it isn't easy. Teens are fighting the odds when they make a commitment to sexual purity. Besides the popular culture screaming "go for it" and some schools distributing condoms to encourage "safe sex," their own hormones are giving them new desires. Our teenage children need our help.

Both boys and girls will seek their identities partly through their sexuality. A young girl will discover quickly that she has the ability to attract a boy's attention, and she will seek to use her wiles, either consciously or unconsciously. A young boy will readily take notice of those wiles and respond by demonstrating a manufactured virility. Though the approach may be different, both enjoy the attention and feelings of importance.

Of course, their new awareness of their sexual identity creates fear and confusion; a parent must be ready to help his or her children accept their developing body and new emotions that accompany it. As a boy enters adolescence, he will struggle as to who he is sexually. He will question his sexuality because the raging chemicals within him confuse his thoughts; the new feelings can turn his new sexual preoccupation indiscriminate. Some entertain thoughts that they may be gay. An alert and savvy parent will help keep the communication open and, at this checkpoint, hold the son to the right angle by helping him understand and sort through his confusion.

In contrast, a girl entering adolescence often recognizes that she has the power to use her body to draw attention to herself, and even to get her way. Usually she will use her body only to catch the eye of that "one and only," not for indiscriminate self-gratification. She finds herself in love with the idea of love, and if not held in check to the right angle will allow someone to use her body in order that she may feel loved. Typically she will not initiate it, but in her vulnerability to peer pressure and her desire to please, she may stumble into sexual experimentation. An early awakening of those feelings that should lie dormant creates for her an overwhelming temptation to give in to her romantic daydreaming.

Don't ignore or become casual about your children's sexuality. Help them through the times of struggle, and coach them on appropriate behavior. Take your son or daughter to dinner or on a weekend outing with the specific goal of addressing right and wrong sexual behavior. Teach him or her how to say no when tempted. Let your child know the painful consequences of giving away what belongs only to his future spouse.

Sadly, if your children don't hear from you about proper attitudes toward sex, they probably won't hear it at all. Give them a healthy standard for normal!

7. SEXUAL ROLES

Try as he may, a man cannot bear children. Try as she may, a woman cannot conceive alone. At the risk of being politically incorrect, Kurt and I are convinced that a man and a woman each has an equally exalted, yet unique role in society. Fatherhood has its own set of demands, as does motherhood. No father can adequately fill the role of mother, nor vice versa. Many single parents do an admirable job, but they certainly wouldn't elect to go it alone if given a choice.

As you help your growing children set an accurate plumb line that will keep them straight as adults, remember that their sexual identity goes beyond sexual feelings and appropriate encounters to filling appropriate gender roles. Boys need to be taught the value of masculine traits and the responsibility of manhood. This includes understanding their responsibility to protect, provide, and lead the home. Girls need to see their femininity as a strength, not a weakness. They need to view bearing and nurturing children as a gift, not a second-rate job. Both need to understand the vital role each can and should play in God's creative design.

Sociologist George Gilder highlights the vital role each sex plays in the great drama of social stability. In his book *Men and Marriage*, Gilder explains that the woman always has a role because she is biologically equipped to bear and nurture children. The man's role, on the other hand, can be taken away by social structure. In fact, he argues, the woman's role in the birth process grants her "sexual superiority" to the man:

> It is the woman who conceives, bears, and suckles the child. Those activities that are most deeply sexual are mostly female; they comprise the mother's role, a role that is defined biologically.
>
> The father is neither inherently equal to the mother within the family, nor necessarily inclined to remain with it. In one way or another, the man must be made equal by society.[2]

How can the man become the equal of woman, as Gilder advocates? Ironically, he becomes her equal by valuing her role as the one who nurtures and his role as the one who provides and protects. Sadly, neither role is wholly clear or necessarily valued today. Gilder describes how modern society has devalued both sexes in the name of "equality." As a result, we have undermined the foundational fabric of a civilized people—clear sexual roles.

In opposition to the general confusion over "normal" and "healthy" sexual roles, parents must establish a right angle where the value of both masculinity and femininity can be defined and modeled. Doing so is not prudish, demurring, archaic, or obsolete. On the contrary, it is vital to a stable and strong society.

WHAT IS NORMAL?

Establishing a plumb line depends on the reliability of the right angle. The right angle must be based on an authoritative, proven, reliable source, one that has been tested and scrutinized by the ravages of time. Such a standard holds true in all settings and transcends cultural bias. It remains relevant across the vale of years. We believe the proper plumb line is the Jehovah God, and the right angle that describes Him and measures truth is His Holy Scripture.

Having the right angle—the Bible—in our heritage chest will create an accurate and normal standard. The right angle gives wholeness to life and is a stabilizing influence to a growing child. Anything contrary to the "normal" (Scripture) is abnormal, and should be identified and recognized as such. Let's give our children that reliable standard.

GETTING PERSONAL

Establishing the "right angle" in your home will not just happen. If you "eyeball" the task, you will move off center. Take some time to make certain you are keeping the job properly aligned.

1. How clearly have you established standards of normal, healthy living for your family? Rate yourself in the following categories. Grade your home from one to five for each, circling the appropriate number. Use the following scale:

> 1 = not at all
> 2 = rarely
> 3 = sometimes
> 4 = often
> 5 = always

Self-Worth—

How clearly do I communicate to my children their individual worth?

| 1 | 2 | 3 | 4 | 5 |

Personal Responsibility—

How well do I instill in my children a sense of personal responsibility?

| 1 | 2 | 3 | 4 | 5 |

Delayed Gratification—

Do I reinforce the concept of earned privilege rather than entitlement?

| 1 | 2 | 3 | 4 | 5 |

Spiritual Exploration—

Do I allow and encourage my children to explore and question spiritual realities?

| 1 | 2 | 3 | 4 | 5 |

Priorities—

Do I consistently model and reinforce proper life priorities?

| 1 | 2 | 3 | 4 | 5 |

Sexuality—

Do I help my children respect and appreciate God's design of human sexuality?

| 1 | 2 | 3 | 4 | 5 |

Sexual Roles—

Do I clearly define, model, and reinforce the value of masculine and feminine roles?

| 1 | 2 | 3 | 4 | 5 |

2. Which most accurately describes your past approach to parenting?

    a. I tend to "eyeball" the job, reacting to what seems right at the time.

    b. I have a clear "right angle" against which I measure my efforts.

    c. I fall somewhere in between.

3. In what other areas do you consider it important to establish a clear "right angle" in the process of giving a solid heritage?

_____   _____

_____   _____

Chapter Ten

THE BEARINGS OF TRADITION

Do you remember the classic musical "Fiddler on the Roof"? It highlights the life of a poor Jewish milkman named Tevye, living with his wife and three unmarried daughters in a small village of czarist Russia around the time of the communist revolution. In the opening sequence, this simple man makes some rather profound observations about the value of tradition to the Jewish people.

"You might say every one of us is a fiddler on the roof—trying to scratch out a pleasant, simple tune without breaking his neck. It isn't easy. . . . And how do we keep our balance? That I can tell you in one word—Tradition! Because of our traditions, we've kept our balance for many, many years. We have traditions for everything. . . . And because of our traditions, every one of us knows who he is, and what God expects him to do."

At this point, the entire cast explodes into song—singing about the role of tradition in their lives. Tevye concludes the sequence with a statement that summarizes their experience.

"Without our traditions, our lives would be as shaky as a fiddler on the roof!"

As the story progresses, much of the tradition Tevye so respected begins to unravel. The custom of fathers arranging marriages for their daughters is challenged by his oldest daughter. The boy she loves asks Tevye for her hand—throwing Dad for a loop. "How can they choose one another? It is the father's role to arrange a husband for his daughter!" But for the sake of his little girl's happiness, Dad approves. After all, the young man was a good, hardworking Jewish boy who at least respected Tevye enough to ask permission.

The second daughter goes a step further, continuing the pattern started by her older sister. She falls in love with a nontraditional Jew. To make matters worse, rather than ask the father for her hand, this boy tells Tevye that they intended to marry with or without his blessing. "How can they tell me? The father must be asked!" Though difficult to swallow, Tevye decides to give his blessing. After all, the boy is still a Jew, even if nontraditional. It is better to bless them and keep a daughter than reject them and lose her. Another step away from tradition is taken. Tevye begins to feel off balance.

Finally, Tevye's third daughter goes beyond the point of tolerance. She falls in love with, and marries, a Christian—a Gentile. He has no Jewish connections whatsoever. Viewing this step away from tradition as too great, Tevye chooses to consider his daughter dead rather than break with such a fundamental part of his identity. The tears flow as his daughter pleads with her father to accept their choice. But it is too much. He walks away . . . heartbroken. His pleasant, simple tune is silenced as the fiddler slips off the edge of the roof.

THE VALUE OF TRADITION

The experience of Tevye and his family is all too representative of what we have done to ourselves as a society. Certainly, there is a place for leaving home—physically and emotionally—and becoming our own person. But there is also a place for building and maintaining a strong sense of identity by passing on a traditional understanding of who we are, and where we have come from. Like Tevye's daughters, we are too quick to break from that heritage in the name of individualism.

Our society has taken pride in its "melting pot" status. It is difficult to attach a single label to Americans because we are a blend of many different ethnic, religious, and social backgrounds. I suppose that is good. But our diversity comes with a price. That price is a gradual loss of identity, of that sense of connection which only comes from being part of something that is handed down from generation to generation. We have replaced the deep roots of legacy with a shallow individualism. In the name of personal freedom, we have enslaved ourselves to an endless pursuit of identity. The problem is that we have rejected the very thing that can tie us to the past and connect us to the future—namely, tradition.

We are not suggesting that all tradition is good. Some traditions can actually undermine a healthy sense of identity. But our generation seems to have burned down the house to get rid of the roaches. Instilling an appreciation for who we are, where we have come from, and how we should live is a vital part of family life. Unfortunately, all too often, it is the part of family life we neglect. We've cut ourselves off from our roots—leaving nothing to nourish our wavering sense of identity.

Our goal is to renew your sense of appreciation for the role of tradition in family life. Not a dry, empty ritual. But fresh, meaningful activities which undergird the process of passing an emotional, spiritual, and relational inheritance between generations. A strong heritage can only be transferred if there is an intentional effort and plan for doing so. It does not just happen. It must be created. As we will see, family tradition can play a vital role in that process.

INHERENT WORTH

The voices of society suggest that man has no innate value. Materialism tells us we are only worth what we possess. Secularism attaches value to what we achieve, not what we are. Humanism says we evolved from an electrically charged pool of slime—making us nothing more than sophisticated beasts. Socialism gives us value only if we contribute to the collective good. Their message is that human life really has no intrinsic value.

No wonder we are suffering from an identity crisis. If life has no meaning, and we have no destiny, then it is easy to buy into the chaos that depresses our society. Do whatever you want! Nothing has value, and nothing matters.

But God sees us differently. He made us in His image. He made us to love and to enjoy Him forever. So, we have eternal value. There is no unimportant individual. We are all of precious value, and God established the traditional family to reinforce that message to His children. But how do we counter the influence of society and instill that sense of value in our homes? How do we give them a strong sense of identity against the odds? In a word, tradition!

PASSING AN IDENTITY

At the turn of the century, American psychoanalyst Erik Erikson coined the term *identity crisis*. He describes the term as the condition of being uncertain of one's feelings about oneself. "This is true," he says, "especially with regard to character, goals, and origin. It occurs especially in adolescence. It comes as a result of growing up under disruptive, fast-changing conditions."[1]

In Deuteronomy 6, Moses is instructed to write and deliver the message from God that certain values were to be delivered and surrendered to generation after generation. "Hand them down," He orders, "as an established custom or practice that has the effect of an unwritten law." That is exactly what traditions are. Traditions are the bearings on which a heritage glides from generation to generation. With many changes in a mobile and developing society, the practice of traditions gives our children stability, dependability, and many great memories. Those three elements can smooth the way as our children move toward adulthood. Such traditions also can make our children want the legacy that we offer.

God knew that Israel's future was indeed going to be fast-changing. He did *not* want them to lose their identity as His beloved people. So He wanted His instructions passed by established, orderly traditions.

If anyone serves as a model of maintaining a strong sense of identity against the odds, the Jewish people do. Think about it. They were scattered for thousands of years, possessing no homeland over which to raise a flag. They endured the hatred and pain of anti-Semitism—including several attempts at racial genocide. Even in this century, European Jews survived near extinction at the hands of a madman named Hitler. Still, despite every reason to abandon or lose their identity as God's chosen people, they have maintained a strong connection with their heritage and with each other. How? One major reason is that the typical Jewish home is rich with tradition.

Every Sabbath, for example, religious Jews set aside an entire day to refrain from work—to take a day off from the grind. They spend time together at home, enjoying one another's company as they observe God's command to work six, rest one. This custom is deeply imbedded in the Jewish soul and reinforces their sense of identity.

The Jewish calendar is filled with festivals, holidays, celebrations, and memorials in connection with key events in the lives of their people. Special activities are planned and carried out in observance of special days. Most of these traditions take place in the home—the setting of choice for passing a heritage. Those reared in an observant Jewish home cannot help but understand their roots as a race, the meaning of their religion, and their identity as God's chosen people.

We Christians can learn much from the Jewish community—in particular, their commitment to passing a heritage from one generation to the next. They have consistently valued and practiced the art of tradition. I believe this is a primary reason that the Jewish people have been able to endure tremendous hardship over the years and still accomplish more than their share of great things.

IDENTITY LOST

There was a time, however, when the Jewish people lost track of their identity. Tradition did not serve them, and they, in turn, served others.

When a devastating famine threatened Israel's existence, Jacob moved to Egypt, where his son Joseph saved the family from certain death. But after the crisis passed, Jacob did not return his family to Canaan where they belonged. Instead, they became slaves to Pharaoh's taskmasters. Rather than build an eternal nation of spiritual influence, they built temporal cities of brick for the pagan Egyptians. Their family life was undermined, and their spiritual celebrations were discontinued. They were in the grip of Pharaoh's powerful fist. In order to mitigate the threat of Jewish influence, Egypt stripped the Hebrews of their identity and began creating a new one for them. They no longer saw themselves as God's special people, but as Egypt's worthless slaves.

Tradition went south . . . oppression was heavy. In fact, it was so heavy, they began to cry out. Jehovah responded.

Moses entered the scene. Ten plagues. Passover. Freedom.

The Hebrews are on their way out of Egypt and find themselves in the wilderness. At first everything seems fine, even exciting. Heading for the Promised Land! Then reality hits. Dusty roads. Blistering heat. Bland meals.

What was their answer to the hardship of desert wanderings?

"Why did we leave Egypt? At least there we had leeks and garlic to eat."

The Hebrew children exposed their true inner selves. Obviously, lack of faith was the main reason they wanted to abandon pursuit of the Promised Land. But why would they suggest going back to Egyptian bondage? After all, there were many other places they could have pitched their tents. What drove them to suggest returning to slavery? In short, lost identity.

Having their spiritual traditions stripped in Egypt effectively cost them their identity. Instead of sons of Jacob . . . instead of children of Abraham and chosen of God, they continued to see themselves as slaves. They were comfortable with bondage, even longed to return to it. Though He gave them every chance, Jehovah found that He could not bring these people into the Promised Land. They had lost sight of who they were.

That generation never regained its strong identity. But by the giving of an ordered law, and requiring it to be passed to their children, the next generation regained a strong spiritual identity.

Something similar happened when the slaves were finally set free in this country. Although the Confederate surrender legally ended slavery, many former slaves went right on living as if nothing much had changed. Oh sure, they had the legal right to get an education, move away, start a business, or any of the things one might do to improve his lot in life. Having a legal right is one thing. Launching out and doing something with that right is another. The former requires a change in legislation. The latter requires a change in identity.

You see, many from the first generation of freed slaves had no idea what to do with their newly given rights. They saw themselves as worthless servants to their masters—nothing more. They lived to satisfy the demands of another. "Life, liberty, and the pursuit of happiness" was the white man's creed. Some families were generations removed from the freedom and pride of African life. They were brought to a strange land, robbed of their customs and stripped of tradition. Their identity was stolen—replaced by a new one—"nigger slave!"

But there were some very notable exceptions—those who refused to embrace an identity of shame. Recognizing their inherent worth as God's children, some began building a new identity for themselves and their people. Though born into slavery, the influence of heroes like Frederick Douglass, Booker T. Washington, Bethune, and Henry B. Delany continue to impact the lives of millions today. Why? Because they launched a new tradition—one that rejects the notion that one man is better than another based upon the color of his skin. They saw and invested in the potential of their people rather than passively accepting the injustice of life.

The message of both the Hebrew children in Egypt and the slaves of America is the same. When people are robbed of their customs and traditions, they lose sight of their true identity. Why else would God's chosen people long for the "good old days" of slavery? Why else would the great-grandson of an African tribal chief view himself as black trash? Put simply, they replaced an identity of worth with an identity of worthlessness. They lost the traditions which tied them to the truth.

Sadly, Christian parents have done the same, allowing the messages of the surrounding culture to dictate their sense of identity. As we stated earlier, God established the traditional family to reinforce a strong sense of identity from one generation to the next. But doing so requires that we incorporate the discipline of tradition into our family life.

UNDERSTANDING TRADITION

There are several characteristics of healthy tradition that should be understood before diving into doing. First, it is important to understand the difference between tradition and ritual. Many people reject the valuable contribution of tradition in reaction to a cold, meaningless ritualism they may have experienced in the home or church while growing up. But there is value in drawing a clear distinction between the two. Here's how we define both.

The Bearings of Tradition

Tradition: *The practice of handing down stories, beliefs, and customs from one generation to another in order to establish and reinforce a strong sense of identity.*

Ritual: *The ceremonial observance of set forms or rites, religious or otherwise.*

While not all ritual is bad, we must be careful with how we use it. Strict ritual can quickly become form without function. Rituals must support the goals of tradition, not the other way around. Traditions, on the other hand, should be reshaped, reformed, and continually refreshed to make them culturally relevant. In fact, every generation will find it necessary to adapt its traditions in order to keep them meaningful and make them its own. Nonetheless, the basic purpose of family traditions remains the same—to reinforce a strong sense of identity in the home.

For tradition to be effective, we must establish the right purpose and content. Without the proper content, our activities will only serve, at best, as entertainment, and at worst, as busy work to salve our conscience. Saying to ourselves, *At least we spend time with our families,* is an attempt to dismiss our feelings of guilt by virtue of that time spent.

Whenever possible and appropriate, traditions should be used as a means to an end. There is value in establishing certain traditions just for the sake of spending time together as a family. But there should also be traditions created that reinforce truth in the lives of our children. Traditions should serve to help our children fulfill Deuteronomy 6:5: "Love the Lord your God with all your heart and with all your soul and with all your strength." That means the spiritual, emotional, and social elements of our lives. As we evaluate our family traditions, we must ask ourselves, "How can we subtly pervade the coming activities with the lesson of God's loving care in our lives?"

THE ART OF TRADITION

Using tradition to instill a strong sense of identity in others is an art, not a science. It cannot be learned by reading a textbook and carefully following a four-step program. Nor can we copy the recipe used by other families. Each home must develop its own unique blend based upon the personalities, purposes, and practices it contains. We offer the following three areas for setting traditions as a general framework to guide your own creativity, not a detailed outline to follow step by step. These areas, however, can help lubricate the bearings of tradition. They also can help you achieve the main goal of tradition: to maintain and pass along a sense of identity and value to your children.

1. EVENTS

Israel did not allow a major event in their history to go unnoticed or unremembered. As a people, they realized the importance of current events that would carry weight. They journalized them. Those days became symbolic. Events over the years became a catalyst for generational passing of the baton.

The night in Egypt when the death angel visited and passed over those who placed blood on the doorposts (Passover) . . . the day when Esther put her life on the line, when she faced down Haman to deliver her people from genocide (Purim) . . . the day when the Temple at Jerusalem was destroyed at the hands of Babylonian conquerors and the Jewish people were forced into exile (Tisha B'Av). These events are celebrated, mourned, and remembered with an eye toward their heritage. They dare not allow future generations to overlook such significant events.

In our fast-paced, highly secularized society, we tend to overlook or downplay the significance of even our most celebrated holidays. How often, for example, have you come to the end of a busy Thanksgiving Day and realized that you had overlooked the process of giving thanks? Other than the obligatory "grace" before digging in, there was no intentional thanksgiving. Caught up in the process of preparing the feast, cleaning the dishes, watching the football game, and forcing down seconds, the family failed to stop and focus on the things for which they had to be grateful.

Or how about Easter—the most meaningful Christian holiday of the year? The eggs get colored, the new dress complimented, and the ham baked. But does the family spend any time at all rejoicing together over the resurrection and the new life available through Jesus Christ? So often, we virtually surrender an opportunity to focus on the content and significance of the occasion.

Don't get me wrong. I see nothing wrong with fun and festivity. In fact, they are part of what make holidays special. But we must not allow ourselves to miss the meaning, or to carry out tradition for its own sake. Again, tradition is the means . . . not the end.

There are several obvious "events" that come upon us every year, at which traditions can, and should, play a major part in family life. Some of the most cherished memories we create in the home include a Christmas tree, a carved turkey, an egg hunt, a birthday cake, or a July 4th backyard barbecue. But there are other less obvious events that provide wonderful opportunities to create family traditions. Here are several. (Many others are listed in the appendix, "Priming the Pump.")

- Celebrate spiritual birthdays to reinforce a child's spiritual legacy.

- Enjoy a special dinner on the anniversary of moving into that new neighborhood; during the dinner reflect upon God's direction in your family's life.

- Host a Report Card Pizza Party every time grades come to celebrate the value of wisdom and learning (The actual grades are less important than recognizing the effort).

- Invite everyone to a periodic Family Date Night, complete with dinner and a show, as a way to rekindle the flame of household harmony and mutual respect.

Get creative. Big events. Small events. Made-up silly events. Regardless of the specifics you may invent, be sure to include events as a major part of your family life. They are a great way to create memories, and essential to the art of tradition.

2. STORIES

In our home, a family gathering is incomplete without the telling and retelling of stories from our past. My children love to hear of the occasions when, as small kids, they pulled off a silly shenanigan, or when they put beads of sweat on our brow. I tell them over and over.

I also love hearing stories of the lives of our parents, grandparents, and great-grandparents. It makes them live in my memory. It connects me to my family's past. It is both fascinating and intriguing. I could bore you with a book full of them, as I'm sure you could with me. But they are for my family. And when we tell them, they are anything but boring to us. They are part of the fabric of our identity.

Perhaps that explains the popularity of the television miniseries *Roots*, one of the most-watched television programs of all time. Based on the popular book by author Alex Haley, the drama followed the lives of one family across several centuries and up-then-down legacy: the pride of eighteenth-century African tribal life, the shame of nineteenth-century American slavery, the struggle against twentieth-century racism, and the triumph of success against the odds. Haley was able to tell the story of his own family line thanks in large part to the storytelling tradition of those who went before. As a child, he sat and listened to aging aunts and grandparents rehearse details of their family tree—telling the story of their roots. Because of that tradition, Haley was able to gain a sense of connection to and pride in his African-American identity.

The Bible is filled to the brim in stories . . . some probably up to six thousand years old. Somebody remembered to pass them down. Somebody knew we needed them. Many times, a particular story from its pages has been the source of strength and encouragement for me! Housed in the words and actions of those episodes are the very reasons we should love the Lord our God with all our heart, soul, and strength.

There are several simple activities you can do to launch a storytelling spree. Flip through an old picture album with your kids. You'll be amazed at how quickly the stories from your collective past will flow. Or how about taking a drive past some of the places where you played as a child, met while dating, or visited with your own parents. What about digging through all that junk in the attic and telling the stories behind different items. Turn "meaningless" pictures, places, and items into an opportunity for "show and tell" or "go and tell."

Another form of storytelling comes through music. Music is an expression and manifestation of the soul. Want to know the moods and values of a particular generation? Study their music. Meshed into the melody lines and harmonic progressions is the message. What is important to them cannot be disguised. What is eating at them cannot be hidden. What is moving them cannot be camouflaged. You can know them . . . if you listen.

For instance, the Psalms, originally set to music, let you know David personally. Listen to Miriam singing a text written by Moses after crossing the Red Sea, and you will be reminded of the miracle-working God. Sneak into the room, and you will overhear Hannah's prayer song after Samuel's birth. Go to Nazareth, and you will marvel at Mary's rendition of Hannah's song. Go to the prison with Paul and Silas, and be encouraged by their jailhouse concert in Acts 16.

Songs have, from the beginning, been a source of passing and identifying a heritage. Our generation logs our own set of values on the grand staff. Anywhere from Stamps Baxter to the contemporary singers of today, music has made a meaningful contribution in my life. Values are memorized and sung over and over. Songs make it possible. Sing with your family . . . supply them with healthy, encouraging lyrics from uplifting music. Utilize this most effective and ancient method of passing a good heritage.

3. CREED

Shortly before his death, the leader of Israel, Joshua, challenged his people. He confronted each of them with a choice.

> Now fear the Lord and serve him with all faithfulness. Throw away the gods your forefathers worshiped beyond the River and in Egypt, and serve the Lord. But if serving the Lord seems undesirable to you, then choose for yourselves this day whom you will serve, whether the gods your forefathers served beyond the River, or the gods of the Amorites, in whose land you are living. But as for me and my household, we will serve the Lord. (Joshua 24:14–15)

Joshua had driven his stake in the ground. He made it known to the entire nation, and more importantly to his own family, that his was a home which would follow God's newly given law. As the first generation to receive God's word in writing, Joshua chose to set the example for his home and nation. "Our family will heed the word of the Lord. That is our standard. That is our creed!"

Let's return to our definition of tradition for a moment. Tradition is the practice of handing down stories, beliefs, and customs from one generation to another in order to establish and reinforce a strong sense of identity. Perhaps the most important aspect of giving a strong sense of identity is passing a clear, credible belief system from one generation to the next. One way of doing so is to establish a family creed—a list of foundational beliefs you will heed and uphold.

At first glance, this suggestion might seem restrictive. A number of parents believe they should allow their kids to decide for themselves what they will believe when they are older. *It would be a violation of my child's free will to dictate a belief system*, the parents reason.

On one level, I agree. It is foolish, not to mention impossible, to mandate adherence to one's creed. We all possess a free will, and that freedom must not be violated. But protecting a child's freedom to choose is one thing. Withholding our parental influence is another. It is imperative that parents drive their stake in the ground—that they intentionally train and mentor their children in the tenets of their faith. Passive silence is not a sign of open-mindedness. It is rather a sign of negligence.

Speaking of negligence, many parents consider the responsibility for passing a belief system to be the exclusive domain of the church. They agree with the value of the creed, but figure the pastor and Sunday school teachers can do the job. However, Mom and Dad must always take leadership in this area of a child's life.

We recommend three steps to establishing a creed for your family. First, *refine your creed*. Make sure you know what you believe and why. Solidify your beliefs about God, truth, the church, the meaning of life, moral absolutes, and any other issues you deem appropriate. *Second, record your creed*. Write it down. Put it someplace where every family member can see and refer to it. *Third, reference your creed*. Talk about it with the family, discussing its tenets. And be sure to make it part of your own life.

A clear creed can become the foundation for your right angle and the content of your impression points. A solid family tradition will include a well-defined creed.

OPENING THE HERITAGE CHEST

It may seem simple to open the Heritage Tool Chest and pull out the items needed. But it's not as simple as spreading the family fragrance or pounding home impression points. You cannot set the right angle and grease the tradition bearings and be assured of a positive heritage. All these items will help, yet they cannot guarantee that your child will accept the heritage. The risk remains that one or more of your children will reject your efforts. For instance, a child can miss, or lose, the meaningfulness of what traditions can give. He may view them as mechanical or manipulative manuevers. Some children will never try, for fear of failing. There is also the risk that rigidity will replace a genuine freshness.

And on your part there may be some hesitation about either the importance or necessity of expending the extraordinary energy to begin and sustain solid traditions in the family. But it is worth it, and no matter what your family background (see Part 3), a positive heritage is possible.

GETTING PERSONAL

Every family has traditions—some by design, others by default. Those who seek to give a strong heritage understand the powerful impact of traditions on the identity of their children. Take a few moments to evaluate the use of tradition in your home.

1. How well have you developed meaningful tradition in your home? Rate yourself in the following categories. Grade your home from one to five for each, five being highest.

Events—

How enjoyable and meaningful have you made periodic events (holidays, game nights, etc.) in your home?

    1   2   3   4   5

Stories—

How often do you tell the stories of your home, giving your loved ones a strong connection to past and present family history?

1   2   3   4   5

Creed—

Does your family have a clear, well-defined belief system that is refined, recorded, and referenced?

1   2   3   4   5

2. If you haven't already done so, prepare a first draft of your family creed—those foundational beliefs upon which your home is established. Once completed, evaluate how well your family traditions have reinforced those beliefs.

3. Identify one idea for each category of tradition which you can implement over the coming months which will serve to establish and reinforce a strong sense of identity with your kids.

Events—

I will plan and prepare for the following event . . .

_____

_____

_____

I will use this event as an opportunity to reinforce . . .

_____

_____

_____

Stories—

I will tell the following story from the life of our family . . .

_____

_____

_____

Creed—

I will refine, record, or reference our family creed by . . .

_____

_____

_____

Part Three
GIVING
THE HERITAGE

He is the happiest, be he king or peasant,
who finds peace in his home.

Goethe

Chapter Eleven

GIVING WHAT YOU DIDN'T GET

It just doesn't seem fair, does it? Some were given a wonderful, healthy, positive heritage—a beautiful gown, a royal robe. Others were handed rags. For some people the process of passing a solid heritage is a natural outgrowth of who they are. Others can't even fathom the experience of positive family living. The good news is that anyone can give a positive heritage. The bad news is that the process of doing so will be much harder for some than others.

You can give what you didn't get. But doing so requires that you move on to a bright future and not remain a victim of your past. It will be hard work, but it will bring great long-term rewards for you and for future generations.

SACRED SACRIFICE

Some "sacrifices" are really self-motivated. We work long hours to be promoted. We endure grueling practice sessions for the chance to shine during the game. We volunteer because we want the praise of others. But the willingness to endure difficulty or personal loss for the sake of others is the essence of charity. It also is the key to giving a strong heritage when you didn't receive one.

I'm too young to have been there, but the moment has been preserved on film for my generation and future generations to visit. I have seen it rerun on television many times. It has a magnetic emotional draw. My eyes stay glued to the events unfolding before me. I wince in anticipation of what I know will occur.

The first segment shows a vast armada of ships sailing under a somewhat overcast sky, headed in concert toward a determined destination. The next picture shows soldiers standing in crowded conditions in what at first seems to be a small room. As the camera pulls back, it reveals they are actually in a landing vessel that will belch them out into shallow water, heading them toward a waiting shore in France, where imminent danger, even instant death, is lurking.

My heart sinks whenever I see the corpses floating in the surf. I see courageous men carrying heavy backpacks and weapons advance toward shore. Some fall . . . some shoot back . . . all realize the odds are great against making it to the base of a cliff where there may be some semblance of safety. Some make it; many don't. Buddy helping buddy . . . panic running unabashed . . . the popping of gunfire dominates the decibels. . . . My heart races as I watch those boys sacrifice what is most valuable so that others might be freed from tyranny.

Thousands made their exit from this earth on the shores of Normandy. The white grave markers near those shores symbolize the string around our collective index finger, reminding us that during World War II our freedom came with a price—a sacred price.

A few years ago I told the story of the painful yet successful Normandy invasion to Paul and Joann, the married couple we met in chapter 2. Both brought children from earlier marriages into their new family. "What does that story have to do with me?" Joann asked. She could not make the connection between soldiers at Normandy and her present family struggles. Paul and Joann were trying to make a blended family work, but neither had a solid reference point. Each had tasted the pain of failed relationships and broken homes before meeting one another and forming a new family.

Though both brought pain into the marriage, both also had hope for something better. Still, Paul and Joann lacked the experiences, skills, or understanding of how to build a solid home life. So the pattern has continued—an unbroken cycle of tyranny. They each asked me the same thing: "How can we give our kids something we've never received ourselves?"

"If the cycle is going to be broken," I answer, "it must start with you. Someone had to be first when we stormed the beaches of Normandy. They sacrificed themselves in order to secure victory. Theirs was not a glamorous role. But they were the true heroes of that battle. They made a sacred sacrifice for the sake of others. That is precisely what you must do for your children and future generations."

Like a roomful of dominoes standing face-to-face, when the tumbling starts, eventually all will fall if someone does not intercede. Someone in this family must pay the price . . . and it is a heavy price. Paul and Joann are determined to put a halt to the cycle that has run several generations and now is flowing into their children's lives. They have realized their responsibility. If they are not devoted to ending it here, it will find its way into their grandchildren's lives. This battle is their "Normandy." They may have to spend the remainder of their lives fighting to create a good heritage to pass to their future generations. Perhaps they may not even get to enjoy it or see its impact. Whatever the outcome, they are in a battle. They are now to the point where they can affectionately call this struggle their "Normandy."

The white grave markers at Normandy are a reminder that those men interceded for us, giving us what they could not enjoy themselves . . . freedom. Paul and Joann's children will never know the full price their parents are paying; but if Paul and Joann succeed, the children will enjoy a freedom they didn't fight for—the freedom to begin their own families liberated from the ongoing pain that could have toppled into their future family lives. They will have the freedom to start fresh, to make their own choices.

ARE SOME PRIVILEGED?

If you are one who was handed rags, your response to the women who received the "gown" and the men who received the "robe" may be cynicism—even anger.

"They were born with a silver spoon in their mouth."

"Their life is easier than mine."

"God is a respecter of persons."

WATCH OUT FOR JEALOUSY

Bitter jealousy can quickly overshadow the lessons to be learned from their experience. Sure, it may be easier for them. OK, you had it harder. Of course the process will be more difficult for you. So what? As Booker T. Washington said in his autobiography, *Up from Slavery*, "Success is to be measured not so much by the position that one has reached in life, as by the obstacles which he has overcome while trying to succeed."[1]

You can successfully give what you didn't receive. Will it be easy? No. Will it be worth it? You bet!

When my wife, Gail, shares how to pass a heritage with others, many "disqualify" her because she was raised in a solid home. "That's easy for her to say. She had a good heritage."

It's true that in many cases an individual who has experienced a particular set of circumstances is more sensitive to others in that situation. A woman who lost her mother in a car accident, for instance, may have a better idea what to say to someone in similar grief than she would if both her parents were living.

But when a man has survived cancer, he doesn't necessarily need an expert in disease to help him return to normal life—he needs someone who can help him with nutrition and other aspects of normal living. For the person who is trying to create a heritage, an individual from a good family legacy can give advice about family health. After all, Gail had the choice to reject the heritage. She had the same pull of the beguiling "ne'er do well" crowd as anyone else. But she chose to keep the good and pass it on. Those who are wise watch and learn from people like Gail, rather than resent them.

You see, the techniques and goals for passing a solid heritage are the same for everyone. They work when used. But the effort required is greater for some than others. The fact that "it's easier for them" is beside the point. Learn from those who do it well. Give the extra effort to make it work for you too. Don't let jealousy distract your focus.

WATCH OUT FOR ANGER

Jealousy, like anger, is a pilferer, robbing us of the very thing we are focused on. Jealousy deceives us into believing he has the rightful place at the forefront. He makes us believe he is our protector when he is really nothing more than a confidence man in a pin-striped suit. Such jealousy will force you to focus on the bad and will only allow you to see half your life—and that half won't be your best, but the broken part.

When we suffer a broken finger, arm, or leg, we quickly forget how good all the other parts of our body feel, focusing all of our attention toward that fractured bone. The same is true with a festering boil, a toothache, or any other painful nuisance. It is our nature to fix the hurt. Even though our eyes, ears, nose, stomach, heart and lungs, liver, kidneys, intestines, spleen, throat, brain, and everything else is healthy, we become consumed with the one area that hurts, and fix it . . . or fixate on it.

The same is true when it comes to trying to pass a heritage. We lock onto what we consider broken. We focus on the negative elements of our past, the failures we've encountered, and the overwhelming nature of the hill we must climb. And all too often, we fixate on the broken part, rather than resolve to set it right. That is tragic.

Jesus Christ is in the business of fixing that which is broken. He frees us from the burden of past pain and failure. As He did with the woman caught in adultery, He sees past our weakness and our inadequacy and gives us something wonderful—a fresh start. Remember the words? "Go and sin no more." Those words were an invitation to start anew—to put the past behind and break the cycle of hurt. Jesus offered that woman an opportunity to break free from the negative and begin again.

He offers us the same opportunity. We can start anew. But as long as we fixate our attention on the broken parts of our heritage, we will never move forward. If we allow parental failures, past abuse, childhood neglect, or any other painful nuisance to dominate our attention, it will keep us trapped in the cycle of pain—and rob future generations of the freedom we might have secured.

STORMING THE BEACH: HOW TO OVERCOME A WEAK HERITAGE

So what is the secret ingredient that enables someone to give what he didn't get? How do we storm the beach, recapturing territory lost to the enemy of a weak heritage? At the risk of oversimplifying a difficult process, there are three key components: prayer, planning, and perseverance.

PRAYER

The first way to overcome a weak heritage is by prayer. You may be thinking, *Oh great, you can't come up with anything more creative, so you say prayer. Why don't you try something a little less trite?*

Hang on . . . I'm flat-out serious here.

In the fall of 1990, Gail and I drove with our son to Orange, California, to help him settle into his first year of college life. Matt had been educated in a Christian school for thirteen previous years. This university was his first encounter with what the secular, humanistic world had to offer. We knew he would be confronted with all that college life in a secular setting would throw at him. Needless to say, we were a bit frightened. He would live in coed dorms, where female "neighbors" often become temporary bedmates. He would be tempted with sinful pleasures that he would not have been introduced to at home. How could we stay involved? How could we stay connected?

Gail fasted every Tuesday for our son, and together we prayed for Matt. We learned more about prayer than ever before. I believe with all my being that this effort was what brought him through unscathed.

By the way, we were right. He encountered all those things we feared . . . but he resisted.

Without prayer, storming the beach becomes a lonely venture. Attacking a weak heritage at times will leave you lonely; prayer gives you strength to face that loneliness. Remember that a weak heritage leaves our children uncovered in the face of enemy fire. Prayer is the vital component in facing this attack.

Today Frank and his wife, Susie, have several grown children—all of whom claim a wonderful heritage. Yet neither Frank nor Susie carried a positive legacy into the marriage. What happened to change things? The two told me that they began the parenting process painfully aware that they had poor role models growing up and that they were clueless when it came to the practical, day-to-day realities of creating a good heritage for their kids. According to Frank, they began to storm the beach through prayer.

"We had to agree early in our marriage that a foundational goal and covenant of our marriage and family was to redirect our heritage, and to understand that it will be difficult for Susie and me, but easier for our children as a result." And what was the starting point? According to Frank, it was prayer. "We began with serious prayer that the Holy Spirit would surround and protect us from any mistakes we might make as a result of the heritage we were given."

Prayer is vital to the process of giving what you didn't get for several reasons. First, you need wisdom, and wisdom comes through prayer. Situations will arise where you have no idea how to respond. That is why the Lord invites us to seek His counsel. "If any of you lacks wisdom, he should ask God, who gives generously to all without finding fault, and it will be given to him" (James 1:5). Or, as Frank put it, "When at a loss, cover with prayer. Answers come!"

Second, you need strength, which also comes through prayer. Giving what you didn't get is a difficult, selfless act. It requires an incredible amount of spiritual and emotional energy. There will be days when you feel like throwing in the towel and walking away from the battle. It is in such times you will need to rest in the Lord's tender, loving care. Remember, "God is our refuge and strength, an ever-present help in trouble" (Psalm 46:1).

Finally, you need release. You may find yourself facing feelings of defeat, anger, even depression. When you make mistakes, which everyone does, you may feel like a failure. Other times you may confront very real anger— even anger at God. "Why did You give me such a bad heritage? It isn't fair!" The physical, emotional, and spiritual exhaustion may even drive you into feelings of despair. Whatever the specific emotions may be, you need time with God. Let Him know how you feel. Cry in His presence. Be honest about how you feel—He can take it. He wants to place His loving arm around you and comfort your pain, calm your fears, and wipe your tears. Let Him.

Why not take a moment right now and talk to God. Ask Him for the wisdom, strength, and release you will need as you try to give what you didn't get.

PLANNING

The old adage "those who fail to plan, plan to fail" applies to the heritage process as much as anywhere else. Good intentions won't get it done. Someday is not soon enough. You must create a plan to drive the actions which make giving a heritage intentional rather than accidental. This is especially true for those who have no solid model to follow, those who seek to break a negative cycle and replace bad with good.

In chapter 14, you will be invited to create your own heritage plan—to walk through several steps to help make sure your family fragrance is sweet, impression points are created, the right angle is established, and traditions are developed and maintained. For now, suffice it to say that a good heritage doesn't just happen; it must be carefully and lovingly planned.

PERSEVERANCE

"Let us run with perseverance the race marked out for us" (Hebrews 12:1).

That's good advice, both for the faith walk and the heritage process. The key to finishing the race is not talent, but tenacity. It does not require experience, but endurance. As Peter Drucker put it, "Some succeed because they are destined to: Most succeed because they are determined to." We must determine that no matter what, come what may, we will stay committed to the task of passing a solid heritage. We are not victims to our past or pawns in the hands of fate. We are soldiers storming a beach, willing to sacrifice our own well-being in order to secure the goal. And sometimes that requires true grit!

Talk to anyone who has successfully broken the cycle by giving what he didn't get, and you'll discover that perseverance is the key ingredient. There are very few immediate rewards. Often it takes years to see the fruit of your labor. And since the long-term impact of your efforts is not clear, it is easy to lose heart. But step by step, day by day, one choice at a time, you are making a difference.

The next wave of troops is counting on you to take that hill!

BREAKING THROUGH

DOING WHAT'S RIGHT

Anyone who has any lingering questions about the possibility of giving what he didn't get needs only to open the Bible to the Old Testament. Chapter after chapter in the books of Kings and Chronicles speak of the men who chose not to follow the footsteps of their wayward fathers. Instead, they sought the Lord. They did what was right in the sight of the Lord. They tore down false religious relics. They plumbed their lives to the right angle and restored the awe and reverence of what was of value to their God.

Each had a choice. Indeed, many of the kings actually continued in their fathers' sins. They perpetuated the generational bias toward evil in the sight of the Lord. Yet, in the midst of it all, a descendant would surface, such as Joash in 2 Kings 12. After a string of rulers who made wrong choices, it is an oasis to read the sentence following his name: "Joash did what was right in the eyes of the Lord." He broke the cycle. He plumbed his life and values against the right angle. He was instructed by Jehoiada the priest. Through Jehoiada he found, and was held to, that right angle. The cycle was broken.

Today, similar stories can be found. Take a closer look at your friends, neighbors, coworkers, and others. The chances are good that you will find people who were given a weak heritage but now are giving something better. If you let them, the example of others can provide you with some much needed inspiration that things can be better.

TWO MODERN EXAMPLES

Jim is one such example to me. You met him earlier. His two older brothers adopted the self-destructive patterns of their father. One of them, following the father's example, eventually sold drugs. He ended up being killed "in the line of duty." Jim's other brother became ensnared by another type of sensual pleasure, pornography. He ended up in jail after getting caught filming children for use in kiddie porn. Jim cares about his family, but he has refused to allow their influence to distract his resolve toward what is right for his wife and baby.

He refused to fixate on the broken part of his life. He began to look toward other families who had a strong heritage and became intensely interested in what they had to offer. He picked up on the right angle. It made sense to him. He realized *his* choices were *his*, and not dealt out for family members to make for him. That right angle he held himself to was the very thing that helped him take his focus off the shattered family life he had grown accustomed to and rally around those elements of the good heritage he had discovered from another family that was in the process of passing a heritage to their own children.

Jim is a modern-day Joash. He is an oasis to my wife and me. After working in the ministry and seeing the many who take the truth and ignore it and sadly come to a shattered end, it is indeed a long, fresh drink of water to witness this modern-day Joash in action.

Sandi is the wife of my best buddy, Sonny McCaskill. A fun-loving but sometimes shy student during college, she drove an old 1950's model Buick that everyone affectionately called "The Ark." It was a lumbering vessel, to say the least. She met Sonny in her third year of college. Sonny noticed her eyes and an inner beauty that radiated through a countenance that rarely revealed any sign of her past. Sonny was practically spellbound. In our dorm room, others talked books and exams. Sonny talked Sandi.

Only after dating her for some time did Sonny learn of her past. Sandi's birth parents had rejected her.

"Many people knew that I was taken in by a foster family who tried to reach out to me. A lot of pain goes along with my story," she would say. Tears sometimes fill my eyes as I am reminded of the things she has recounted to me, the absence of her original parents and the emotional distance from her foster parents.

If anyone had the "OK" to draw into a shell . . . if anyone had the right to chuck it all and focus on the broken, it would be Sandi. "But I refuse" she told me. "I am determined to beat the past. I am determined to voluntarily fight my own 'Normandy.' It has been a lifelong battle." She continues, "There have been times I ran for safety at the base of the cliffs. There have been times when it seemed the enemy was just too powerful . . . the urge to give up, to give in . . . was very great."

But she didn't.

Sandi married Sonny after dating him for a year; later they had children, though tragedy visited there, too. Their first child died at birth. Sandi has fought to create a heritage for her two living children. She has continually sewn that Victorian wedding gown and royal robe to hand down. "I refused the rags that I was handed," she will willingly tell you.

Sandi McCaskill makes a strong case for "giving what you didn't get." Despite Sandi's past, her two grown children, Mark and Lori, received a strong heritage and a beautiful gown and royal robe. They now have the opportunity to pass to future generations those new garments that Sandi and Sonny handed to them. If you did not receive a strong heritage, do not despair. Just as Jim and Sandi have done with their own families, you too can pass on a strong cord to your children.

Chapter Twelve

EXTENDING
THE HERITAGE

I f you want to observe a success story in action, you should meet Olivia. She is one of those people who attracts others to herself like a magnet. She has the gift of encouragement, and she uses it. And yet, if anyone has reason to feel discouraged, it is Olivia. She was given a very weak heritage—spiritually, emotionally, and relationally. As I described earlier, hers was a childhood of neglect, rejection, and pain. But she has overcome the past and is building a wonderful heritage for her own family today. Doing so has required that she storm the beach and break the cycle.

Growing up in a single-parent home with five siblings would have been difficult enough for Olivia. Adding to the stress, she watched as her four brothers and sister dealt with the ongoing fallout of family collapse—memories of Daddy hitting Mommy, the confusion, the fear, the rejection, several serious bouts with suicide-level depression, and one attempt to actually carry out the suicide compulsion.

Olivia had little time with her mother, who was working days and attending school in the evenings. There was no time, money, or energy to braid her hair, buy pretty party dresses, or talk about boys. Even when they were together, there was more shouting than sharing. Of course, there was no healthy male role model in the home. No one to call her "daddy's little sweetheart" or teach her to ride that first bicycle.

Olivia was given no positive spiritual heritage. Olivia's mother had rejected her Catholic roots. Her emotional and relational legacy was very weak. Home was a place to fight, not a place to rest. In short, Olivia was handed rags.

A HELPFUL FATHER FIGURE, A CARING COUPLE

During her early teen years, Olivia developed a strong friendship with Darcee, the daughter of a local pastor. Darcee's father was a strong yet gentle man who deeply loved his family and showed it. It wasn't long before Olivia began to spend more and more of her time at Darcee's house, observing and experiencing firsthand what a healthy family could be. They didn't mind at all. In fact, they took her in as part of the family. There was more than enough love to go around. They extended their heritage to her, giving Olivia some stability in the present and a model for the future.

Years later, Olivia and Darcee, still best friends, packed their bags and headed off to college together. They attended the same small Christian college in Southern California. While there, Olivia hooked up with two faculty members, husband and wife. Like Darcee's parents, they invited Olivia into their home and into their lives.

Olivia watched that couple carefully preserve and pass the gown they had been given to their own daughter. Olivia learned the secret to creating a sweet-smelling family fragrance and the value of meaningful family tradition. She saw them using impression points with the children and setting the right angle straight. They invited Olivia in and extended their heritage to her. Today they find no greater reward than watching as she does the same for others.

EXTENDING YOUR HERITAGE

Olivia understands the value of what we've labeled "The Extended Heritage." She received it from two families during critical periods of her own life. They gave her something she would have never otherwise received—a glimpse of what a heritage can be and an understanding of how to give what she hadn't received at home . . . which, by the way, is the essence of our definition. Put simply . . .

The Extended Heritage is the process of sharing your heritage with those who may not have a strong heritage of their own.

Those who have discovered and mastered the art of giving a strong heritage should extend that blessing to others. It is a wonderful gift that should be shared, not hoarded. And as we've discovered, when you give it, you get even more in return. As Jesus taught, "Give, and it will be given to you. A good measure, pressed down, shaken together and running over, will be poured into your lap. For with the measure you use, it will be measured to you" (Luke 6:38). Practice the art of giving a heritage to those outside your family, and watch this promise of receiving transpire. The blessing will come back at you in many terrific, unexpected ways.

Tom is standing on the platform at church with a row of fifth- and sixth-grade boys beside him. He listens as they quote Scripture learned in their Wednesday evening AWANA program. I feel a pride welling up within me and a lump in my throat. Though no blood relation, Tom has been in our family for years. He is a big, stout young man, and his army training is showing tonight as his charges behave well and know their Bible verses.

My mind goes back to all the holidays he spent at our home. On every family video of Christmas for the last eight or nine years, Tom is conspicuously present. That is because he is a part of our extended clan. We saw in him a desire, a leaning toward making right choices.

We gave. He responded.

We gave more. He responded.

We reached out further. He responded.

And that scenario over the years has developed into our extending to Tom the heritage we delivered to our birth children. We created intentional impression points for him. We waited on Christmas until Tom could come over to open gifts. His was always under the tree. He participated in Thanksgiving dinners with us. He ate Sunday dinners in our home. When he graduated from high school and entered the military, we stayed in contact and looked forward to his coming home. He asked a lot of questions. We engaged in a lot of conversations. He made the right choice in marriage, and we have an extended "daughter-in-love" (as my wife calls her) and, now, an extended grandson. We still do the holidays together, and he and Kristin are prepared to pass a good heritage on to Kale, his son . . . his firstborn. Tom is the heir of our extended heritage. I believe it is in safe hands. That's where that pride is originating from . . . and I'm going to let it run free tonight.

LESSONS FROM AN OLD COIN AND FROM JELLY BEANS

Years ago I obtained a coin no bigger than a dime. Made of copper, the coin had the words "our Navy" inscribed on the back; the front featured a side view of someone I do not recognize but suspect to be a famous woman. She is surrounded by stars on the outer circumference, except where the date is stamped. That date speaks volumes about the coin, because it was minted during the Civil War—1863. One thing that is conspicuously missing on the coin is its worth. Flip the coin all you like, and you will find no denomination . . . no value stamped on its face.

I stuck the coin in my pocket and drove to the mall to allow a dealer, a coin expert, to price the coin. His reply was surprising and intriguing. The coin was worth about fifteen dollars if I wanted to sell it to the dealer, but back in 1863, its value depended on its owner. If the owner was a good barterer, its value increased. If its owner wasn't, it could be worthless. The coin was worth whatever one could get out of it.

For some, it may have been worth a loaf of bread, for someone else, a gallon of milk. Others may have traded it for a basket of eggs, but if you were a smooth talker and a cunning trader, maybe a goat or pig. It was all up to the owner.

I kept that coin. Every time I look at it, I recall a lesson in value: Its value must be measured by something external to itself—its owner.

Sitting on the conference table in my office is a large container of jelly beans. They aren't there for me or my staff. They are there for all my knee-high pals. I have a soft spot in my heart for kids. After a service, at some point, we all go in to enjoy a simple jelly bean. The wide-eyed thrill permeates their pudgy faces. That small favor invokes reactions I could never forget. I get grins . . . I get hugs . . . I get kisses . . . what I really get is pure enjoyment.

One day I was standing at the back of the sanctuary chatting with a few church members when I felt a tug on my coattail. After finishing my sentence, I looked down into the face of a little cherub with thick glasses that magnified his big, blue eyes. He spoke with a lisp, adding to his childish charm. "Pathtor," he shyly started, "I've nevuh been in you offith." He accented "nevuh" with a high-pitched tone.

"Would you like to go in and see my office, Joshua?" I asked, knowing his answer and his motive already.

"Could I?" he shot back, still in that high-pitched tone as he was on the edge of euphoria.

There was no set value stamped on that little one's face. He is a priceless work of God's art. Thank God he and the others who visit me weekly all have parents who know the significance of a good heritage. But what about those who don't? What about those who are part of homes bent on giving a bad heritage? Does that mean that they have diminished worth? Of course not!

When we as adults give children who are not our own offspring our time and love, we help them on the road to a better heritage. Like my Civil War token that some paid dearly to own (though others gave very little), we can choose to attach high value to their children's lives. Whether it's inviting them in to share a jelly bean or taking them to the local playground on a fall afternoon, our participation with them tells them they have value.

WHO CAN GIVE AN EXTENDED HERITAGE?

To answer the question "Who can give an extended heritage?" I need only look at the many family members I meet in my travels. They believe exactly about the heritage as I do. They want to give it, and they are shaping their children accordingly. The job they are accomplishing is heartening. In addition to parents, some are aunts and uncles, grandparents, and single adults. Others are childless couples, teachers, and the list goes on. Yes, the answer to the question "Who?" is any relative or friend —anyone who knows what a heritage is and wants to extend that heritage past themselves into the lives of others.

Let's look at how four kinds of people can give an extended heritage: grandparents, aunts and uncles, childless couples, and teachers.

GRANDPARENTS

God bless grandparents who are just exactly that . . . *grand parents*. Some look at that stage of their lives as the time to get away from kids. "I raised mine, now you raise yours." If the empty nest means we are supposed to abandon the lives of our children and their children and only offer a small, paltry, insignificant amount of time with them, then maybe we should be called "grandpittance" and not "grandparents." Many grandparents, full of love for their children and their children's children, recognize the great opportunity to teach and inculcate values by passing them on to their third generation.

When things were tense or a trifle boring at our house, our kids took off to Grandma's. They were pampered. They weren't pressed to perform household tasks. She filled up their bellies. They napped. Yet our values were enhanced and lived out through their lives. Perhaps taught more subtly there, yet taught indeed. Grandma Ledbetter was hammering home the heritage she had already given me.

The "grand" in front of the title of parent simply means a parent higher in rank. *Parent* is a word that means to produce and maintain. Being a grandparent means one has been promoted in rank, given more entitled authority to maintain what has been produced.

Grandparents, your influence can give a heritage beyond even your immediate family. If you have no grandchildren around, adopt some. Look for couples who are lost and befuddled in their job of parenting. Look for children of single parents. Look for kids unintentionally abandoned by overworked, overextended parents, and offer that extended heritage. Plan some impression points with them. Their mom and dad may be more occupied with their occupation than inculcation of their true values. What a great opportunity for you to make a compelling impression.

AUNTS AND UNCLES

Dan sat through the men's retreat as I spoke on passing the heritage, wide-eyed and glued to the subject matter. I knew I had strummed a chord on his heartstrings. I felt good about it. *Maybe one more man to catch the vision of the magnitude of his job.* So, you can imagine how I responded when I found out he and his wife could have no children.

"Don't be surprised," he said. "I have a question I need to ask."

We walked down a hallway to the end of the chapel and sat down. Dan was a proportionately large man. The dark flesh around his eyes was turning red and tears were about to follow as he choked out the details of his sister's children. She had lived an abused life, was abandoned by the father of her children, and now had appealed to Dan for some kind of help. Not financial. Just support. He had turned her away.

Boy! Did I ever strum a chord on his heartstrings. I think I played an entire song.

Dan has since contacted his sister and is intensely involved in the lives of his nieces and nephews. He is determined to give them a chance to have a heritage. Dan is in ministry full-time now and is a true believer in the extended heritage.

You may be able to help your brother or sister. In fact, often other members of the family can be part of an extended heritage given to the children of relatives. Aunts, uncles, cousins—whatever relation you are to children—you can extend and connect . . . and you should!

SINGLES

Donna Goede has long, straight, blonde hair and a shy smile that assumes nothing but only reveals the true character of her sweetness. And if she read this, she would turn beet red with discomfort for being singled out. Donna was a very smart and capable young lady who attended the college and career class I taught in the early 1980s. Even though she was tall, thin, and very striking, I never saw her interest in any young man blossom. Her interests at the time lay in education. Once in a while she would show up at Bible study with her sister's children, a preschool boy and girl. If anyone has mentored me about the value of singles creating and passing a heritage, it is Donna Goede.

One group of people is, perhaps, more stereotyped than any other group. Not because of ethnicity. Not because of gender. Not because of education or their social status. They are typed because they remain single. For whatever cause, they choose to live their life without a mate. Because of their choice, they sometimes are looked on as damaged goods.

But what a fertile ground to create, grow, and extend a heritage to others! The great apostle Paul is found in this group. He stated that in his opinion, to stay single is the best option. He wished all could live as he was. He was not bound or encumbered by the restraints of caring for other immediate family members. He was free to pick up and go at the whim of His God, to accomplish numerous missions for His kingdom.

Donna made the same choice. At a young age, she was put into a home for juveniles because her mother was unable to cope with rearing seven children alone. I remember her as a young teen when she began to attend our church in southern California. I knew she had a love for her sister's two children. I could see it in the way she handled them.

Her sister was a drug addict and couldn't manage a decent home for those kids. So the state of California stepped in and threatened to take them away. Donna asked for and received them into her home.

The children were ecstatic about the possibility of living with Donna. They held the thrill in check as the adoption was attempted. Only after it was negotiated did they begin to call her "Mom." Later, her sister gave birth to another baby. This one is slightly retarded. Donna also adopted her.

Not long ago my wife and I traveled to the Los Angeles area to visit some old friends. While entering a popular local restaurant, we met Donna as she was ready to leave with two of her adopted children, Charlene and Donovan. Donovan is tall; he towers over his mom. Charlene is a beautiful young lady. Both are actively involved in their church.

Donna's church family worried about her, because having put everything she earned into raising these kids, the only car she could afford was a "clunker, " a beat-up jalopy. She drove forty-five minutes one way to work every day. She has sacrificed her entire life to give a legacy of love to the kids. It had to be hard. Who encouraged her? Who did she talk to when she had doubts? Who did she bounce things off when parenting became a frustration? I don't know, but I know she has been a successful parent. Last year Charlene graduated from a local high school with top honors. Donovan is on track to do the same next year.

As a single lady, never married, Donna was named Mother of the Year by her church in May 1995.

Indeed, singles can also extend a heritage. Shake off the stereotype! Your influence can give a heritage to someone beyond your immediate family.

CHILDLESS COUPLES

Few things are as painful as the realization that, though you have a wonderful heritage to pass and a deep desire to do so, infertility or miscarriage has robbed your home of those who would have received it. The hurt of empty arms is very real. Many allow themselves to become trapped in a cycle of anger and despair. But childless couples do have another option. They can go ahead and give that heritage away to people like Olivia and Tom.

If you find yourself in this situation, you still can extend your legacy to those outside the four walls of your home. You and your spouse can turn the void into a victory. Redirect your passion to the process of inviting others into your circle of love and investing in their lives.

TEACHERS

Apart from parents, few people have as great an influence on the impressionable years of childhood as do teachers. Schoolteachers and Sunday school teachers in particular have a tremendous opportunity to extend a heritage to other people's kids.

It was in the classroom that Gail first began investing in Olivia's life. Later, Olivia began extending that second-hand heritage into the lives of other kids in the classroom when she became a teacher herself. One of her favorite "projects" has been a lovely young lady named Nicole. She first met Nicole as a fifth-grade student. Nicole had an eagerness to learn and a willingness to love. Olivia gave, and Nicole responded. Olivia gave a little more, and Nicole continued to respond. Years later, the two still keep in touch, and their teacher/student relationship has blossomed into a deep love and friendship. Olivia is giving what she received, and receiving from Nicole in return.

Teachers, never underestimate the powerful influence you can have in the lives of those you instruct. As you take extra time to reach out to those little lives around you, you become a model and can strengthen a heritage cord for future leaders.

HOW TO GIVE AN EXTENDED HERITAGE

Countless people all around you would welcome an extension of your heritage. If you can't find someone, the problem is a lack of vision, not the lack of necessity. But how do you go about starting the process? Obviously, just walking up to someone in the mall or on the street corner and asking, "Hey, want a heritage? I've got one to pass along" is not going to work. But people who know they have a need and are looking for an answer and an identity often frequent places where they feel their need might be met.

The way to give an extended heritage is to locate those places. Here are four ways to find young people wanting to develop a heritage, if only they knew the benefits and had someone to ask them: (1) ask at your local church, (2) write letters, (3) consider adopting a child, and (4) take time for children who have only one parent at home.

1. ASK AT CHURCH

She was pretty and talented. Yet at age twenty-six, Darlene fell face forward and drowned in her own vomit. Her parents were devastated at the death of their only child, whose future shined so brightly. However, they did not allow bitterness to take root, as they continued to help other women. For Doris Cook, there are many other young women out there who need nurturing. The heritage her daughter no longer needed is extended to any woman or young girl in the church who wants a piece.

Doris and Vertus, her husband, offer their time to many women in our church, even my wife and youngest daughter. Gail calls Doris "My Other Mother," and Doris watches our youngest daughter when we have an engagement. The Cooks make special plans for her: certain dishes to cook for and with her, games they traditionally play just with her, crafts they plan for her visits. And they always mention how much she's grown and mark it on a door facing.

Church is a great place to go if you are in need of giving, or receiving, that extended heritage. It's a great place to connect. In churches across America, I have found couples like the Cooks helping youngsters. You and your spouse can too.

2. WRITE LETTERS

The power of the written page cannot be overstated. Well written thank you's or congratulations can have a profound impact upon people's lives. My son, Matthew, received a letter soon after the untimely death of his favorite cousin that illustrates this point. The letter, which continues to have a major impact on him, was from his cousin Chris's parents. It read:

Dear Matt:
    It sure was good to see you again, to be able to have some fellowship and shoot some "hoops," such as it was when I shot them. If my living was dependent on making those bas-

kets, you can see I would have starved to death by now. I sure hope you do well in school this year. You guys be sure to drive carefully while you are on the road.

You probably know that Chris considered you to be one of his favorite cousins. He cherished the time he could spend with you, and it was always special to him. It may have been because of all the mischief the two of you got into in kindergarten. Anyway, he really liked having you for a friend and cousin. God took him and left you behind. I don't know why God considered his life over, and that yours should continue. I do know that since He did, He means for your life to have purpose to it. Matt, life was not meant to be a time of rest, relaxation, or fun and games. It was meant to have focus, purpose, and direction. God has blessed you with a keen intellect, talents, good looks, health, and material means. He has given you at least five talents (like in the Bible). Evidently, He is expecting great things from you. If you will take these five talents and place them in God's hands, at His disposal, to do with them whatever He pleases, He will give your life that direction. God has left you here because He has a work for you to do. I know that you are a Christian and that you will again see Chris someday, but when you see him, be sure that you have done all you could with what you have been given for the Lord. Don't have to hang your head in shame because of a wasted life.

Chris' life was short, but it had purpose and direction. At the time of his death, he had not yet perceived the call of God on his life, so he started in a direction, with permission to the Lord to change his direction anytime He pleased.

The reason I am telling you this is because it would please your Aunt Bettye and me very much to see you give your life wholly over to the Lord's control. That does not mean you have to be in the Lord's work full-time, but that you would be in His control full-time. That would make you successful. You may die a pauper, but you would die a success. That is the only kind of success that counts.

God bless you, Matt. Come to see us when you can. The invitation will always be open.

With love,
Uncle Don & Bettye

They sent a similar letter to my daughter Becky.

Obviously, you must be careful what you say and to whom you say it when you use letters as a means of influencing others. Many use letters to avoid interpersonal communication, rather than to enhance it. Others use letters to say what is on their mind, appropriate or not. But if done right, letters can be a powerful tool for having an extended impact.

One man's life and stories have made deep impressions on my life. If he weren't so trustworthy, some of his stories would not be believable: visions, spirit encounters, even after-death experiences. If I had read these stories from anyone else . . . well, I might not accept them. He wrote me that he had been in and out of jails and had assassins after him like some royal sheik or president. Every place he went, people tried to discredit him. He was a real believer in letters. I have some of them in my possession. I take them out every day and peruse at least a part of them. They do me a great deal of good.

I especially like the one he wrote to the Philippians. That particular letter of the apostle Paul is special to me. His heritage is passed to me on those pages. His words are deep.

No, the influence of letters cannot be overstated.

3. CONSIDER ADOPTION

Roy sang in barbershop quartets and his wife, Lindy, was interested in piano. To an outsider, it seemed that music may be all they had in common. My wife and I happened to be going to the same destination as they were one day, so we followed behind them in our car. For the thirty miles we drove, she looked out her passenger-side window and his eyes were on the road. Not one glance at each other . . . not one noticeable exchange of phrases. Yet, they were both talkers in a crowd of peers. So one day when I felt brave, I asked Roy about the relationship. He honestly told me there wasn't much of one.

Early on a Saturday morning in the early 1970s, we received a call from a local hospital. To our complete surprise, it was the secretary for the man who owned the small community hospital.

"Last Monday a newborn girl was abandoned in a linen basket here at the hospital. The mother has died, and no relatives can be found. The doctor told me to call you and ask if you and your wife would like to have the baby."

Our children had not yet been born, but we did want our own if we could. How could we turn this child away, though? As we prayed, God revealed. Roy and Lindy, who were childless and could have no children, gladly took the precious bundle. Both were recipients of a good heritage, yet would have let it die until the little girl came along. As they focused on the baby, extending their name and heritage to her, their relationship breathed new life. Today they have a vibrant relationship and love their daughter, Regina.

I wonder how many childless couples have a great heritage to give, but have never thought of extending theirs through adoption or even through a friend relationship. Wouldn't it be thrilling to give what you received to someone who has not been offered a good heritage, and probably will not receive one either? It does not have to be blood relatives, as in Dan's experience. It just takes a desire to spend the effort of involvement.

4. HELP A CHILD IN A SINGLE-PARENT FAMILY

The number of single-parent homes in America continues to increase. Caused by divorce, abandonment, out-of-wedlock births, and premature death of a spouse, single-parent families experience a real strain financially. But the children also suffer socially, spiritually, and emotionally. The effects of growing up in a single-parent household can't be averted, but they can be mitigated. The greatest help can come from intact families.

By engaging ourselves in the effort of helping these families, the children of single parents can receive the

benefits of an extended heritage. Inviting them to participate in your traditions will show them how family roles
operate. A boy with an absent father can be given the OK
to grow up and be a man. A girl can see the value she
brings into the family and be taught her worth and significance. It's all so inexpensive, yet so priceless. Really, what
price is too high for a youngster to be given the opportunity to grow up with proper "fleshed out" knowledge of
real living?

REAPING THE REWARDS

Bob Fitzgerald thought his father, George, would help
him during high school, and George fully intended to do
so. But a fatal heart attack struck down Bob's father as Bob
entered high school in a Deroit suburb. His mother, Cin-
dy, would have to go it alone, and she tried to manage the
father role as best she could. Soon, though, the father of a
neighborhood girl whom Bob liked began to offer him an
extended heritage. Louis, age thirty-six and the father of
four daughters, recognized an opportunity and seized it.
He opened his house to Bob, letting Bob see a father in
action. Louis answered questions, and he taught values
by living the example Bob needed to see. Bob was interested in Louis's daughter, Gail, a pretty, bubbly girl, but
he also greatly appreciated Louis.

Eventually Bob followed in Louis's footsteps and became a Christian. After high school, Bob attended a Christian university and then joined the pastoral staff at a large
church on the West Coast. Recently Bob wrote this tribute
to Louis Hover in a special edition of their church paper:
"When I reflect on my years at Temple, my thoughts are
more of relationships, rather than events. One of the first
relationships that comes to mind is the Louis Hover family. It was Louis's daughter Gail who invited me to Temple,
and because of her efforts, I established the most important relationship in my life when I received Jesus Christ as
my Savior. Louis Hover was a great example to me of dis-
cipleship and Christian living."

Gail accompanied Bob one time to a college banquet. Today she and Bob are good friends—and Gail has become Mrs. Otis Ledbetter. Meanwhile, Bob still regards Louis Hover as almost a second father.

Like Louis Hover, you should be ready to interact with a child. Look for opportunities to help relatives' and neighbors' children. You will encourage them, and who knows, you may be able to offer an extended heritage as well.

Chapter Thirteen

MIXING THE HERITAGE

I am not a cook. The biggest joke around our house comes when I offer to prepare dinner. Everybody knows that means either we are dining out, or we are having scorched grilled cheese sandwiches and chicken noodle soup from a can. Several of my attempts have cramped my wife's sides with laughter. My self-image really suffers trauma in the kitchen.

My friend Steve, on the other hand, is a gourmet cook. He lives to prepare a meal to excite the taste buds . . . to create a plate so perfect that the recipient of his masterpiece will find his senses snapped to attention.

"Tell me about creating the perfect soufflé," I asked, curious about how one prepares a major league entrée. Here is what I learned as he walked me step-by-step through the process.

BLENDING A SOUFFLÉ

The generic cheese soufflé starts with butter, flour, eggs, and cheese. Separate the whites and yolks of the eggs first, then melt the butter and beat the yolks . . . mix it together with the flour. Add finely grated cheese and slowly heat and stir until it creates a foam on top. Then beat the whites until they peak like a thick whipped cream. One-third of the cream is added to the previous mixture, then begin mixing by folding. (I even learned what folding is.) The remaining two-thirds of the whites go in the bottom of a prepared casserole dish with tin foil around its edges to add five or six inches to the height. I guess that is to allow the soufflé to rise.

So here we are: egg whites on bottom and the cheese sauce slightly cooled. Now pour and fold in the sauce, and place the dish in the oven for forty-five minutes. (You're smiling at me.) Watch it rise to perfection. (I hear you applauding! Thanks, it helps my self-image.) We have it—a perfect soufflé.

During the process, the blending, the mixing, the right temperature, and the properly measured ingredients are all vital. Overheat the cheese sauce, underwhip the whites, or overmix the egg whites and cheese sauce, and the cheese dish will turn out hard. While the soufflé is baking, you dare not open the oven door and create temperature changes. And a sudden small gust of wind or a banging door will collapse the rising soufflé. In short, creating a cheese soufflé isn't at all like making scorched cheese sandwiches and canned chicken noodle soup. It is much more fragile.

Believe it or not, preparing a cheese soufflé is similar to giving a heritage. Each is a delicate task. You need the right mixture, a good sense of timing, clear focus, and a true-grit determination. A jolting, vibrating crisis can collapse the whole thing. To do it right requires the skill of a gourmet parent, rather than a "fricasseeing wanna-be."

BLENDING TWO HERITAGES INTO ONE

Every marriage blends two unique individuals into a single family unit. Each brings a different set of experiences, a different view of "the right way," and differing expectations into the relationship. Each also carries a unique heritage mix across the threshold. Some of these differences are what make the relationship interesting and exciting. Others can lead to severe disagreement and conflict.

When children enter the picture, the plot thickens. As one man said, "I thought I finally had nestled into a semi-comfortable position in my relationship, until someone came along who could 'out selfish' me." When baby makes three, the two had better unite as one. That leads us to a very important question: How does a couple blend two heritages into one?

Some relationships bring religious differences. "Will we raise the kids Baptist or Presbyterian?" Others bring regional, cultural, or ethnic differences into the marriage. "Will we serve grits or bagels at breakfast?" Differences can be minor—what a child should wear—and major—how to discipline the children. Add multiple marriages and children from previous mates, and the mixture becomes delicate indeed. Whatever the specifics, whether trying to blend minor differences or major disagreements, it is vital that Mom and Dad figure out a way to give a single, united heritage to the kids. And it won't just happen. It must be planned.

Most of us enter the bond of marriage and the job of parenting with nary a thought toward the differences we may encounter over big and small issues alike. But they *will* impact the heritage-passing process. If we never intentionally address the differences, we cannot successfully blend our heritage.

There is no magic formula or deeply profound secret to creating a blended heritage. It simply requires a willingness to invest the time and effort needed to make it happen. We recommend the following recipe.

1. Honestly examine your own past heritage. It has had, and will have, a direct impact upon your expectations, behavior patterns, and attitudes. Hopefully, you've already walked through this exercise earlier in the book.

2. Compare your past heritage to your mate's past heritage. It is best to grab some paper and list the characteristics side by side to highlight any dramatic differences. If you have never done so, talk about your upbringing with your spouse. You may discover things about each other that you never understood or appreciated before.

3. Discuss the areas of your combined heritage that seem solid. Then discuss those that appear weak and need to be strengthened. Some areas may need to be completely replaced. You may be surprised just how many negative characteristics of your mixed heritage neither of you wants, but both of you cause. Each partner may also discover aspects of his or her own legacy that he or she has stubbornly insisted should be modeled, but that actually cause more harm than good. Talk about them. Some simple, honest communication can work wonders for the blending process.

4. Write down the characteristics that you both wish to see included in the heritage given in your home. Come to agreement, even if it requires compromise (and it will). Give and take, so that your children can get something worth taking.

After completing the above four steps, create a united plan for making your mixed heritage goals a reality. Again, talk is good, but action is better. Complete the "Planning Your Heritage" exercise in chapter 14 to launch your efforts.

ABOUT BLENDED MARRIAGES

One of the most popular TV family shows in the 1970s featured a woman with three daughters who married a widower with three sons, creating the "Brady Bunch." This loving family offered cute laughs and good moral lessons, but the program remains one of the least realistic television shows of all time.

Week after week, this blended family illustrated how easy it is to resolve any and all family conflicts in neat, thirty-minute segments. Such a blended family does not exist.

"The Brady Bunch" is life as we want it to be, not as it is. In truth, one of the most difficult ventures anyone can undertake is trying to make a blended family work. The goal of creating a healthy mixed heritage confronts its greatest challenge when two family units merge into one.

Remember Paul and Joann, the couple who blended their families from previous marriages? When they came to me for counsel, the condition of their home was extremely sensitive. In an already delicate atmosphere, one of the older daughters introduced pornography to the younger children. Then, theft and threats raised their ugly heads. Internal friction aggravated those problems, and the family's emotional and social elements seemed on the verge of collapse.

Rather than dealing with the symptoms, we began exploring the foundation upon which Paul and Joann were attempting to build a family unit. Was there a united heritage plan, or were they passive victims to past dysfunction?

1. MAKING A LIST

As we considered the past, Paul and Joann soon recognized their own heritages had been mixed; some good elements, more bad. That's the first step to blending a heritage—evaluate your own. That is necessary whether you and your spouse are celebrating one continuous marriage or you have been remarried and must blend traditions and experiences from two family units that have joined into a new entity. The goal is to have a united heritage plan, and it begins with pencil and paper.

If you are a parent of a blended family, there are additional factors to mixing a heritage; these are discussed on pages 231–34. But these three steps, beginning with "Making a List," apply to all families, from single-parent and blended families to the more common two-original-parents families. In your goal to create a single, united heritage plan, first sort out what is there from your own past. Sit down together and make a list.

Next, you "toss out the bad." That is, you acknowledge the negative elements of your heritage, express your desire not to pass them on, and choose to keep the good elements. When we replace the bad with good, we are establishing a new pattern for the "Victorian wedding gown" we want to pass on to our daughters (and the royal robe to our sons).

Significantly, both the husband and wife should know about the weak aspects of each other's heritage, so they can understand the spouse's struggle and help the mate with support and sensitivity. Each should know and be committed to the strengths of their own and the other's heritage that they want to perpetuate to their children. Thus, making a list is a crucial aspect of blending the family, and I urge you and your spouse to do so.

Let's look at how to do that by following Paul and Joann through the procedure. They began by making a list of what each brought into the marriage.

In listing their spiritual legacies, they saw neither had a very solid foundation, and both had rejected much of what they had been given. Both Paul and Joann brought a moderate to weak spiritual legacy into the marriage. Here are their lists:

Our Spiritual Legacy

Paul's

- Spiritual realities were introduced, but with limited personal involvement. I later rejected religion.

- I was taught to be spiritual because people were watching. "Don't embarrass us," my parents told me.

- Spiritual activities were sporadic and intermittent.

- My parents taught me that spiritual issues were private—not to be shown.

- They clarified the difference between right and wrong.

- God was personal, but spirituality was separate from the practical.

Joann's

- I saw my parents' spiritual lives as hypocritical, with superficial personal commitment. So I rejected spiritual realities.

- I was taught to be spiritual because people are watching. "You can't shame the family," they said.

- We had only occasional spiritual activities in the family.

- My parents rarely discussed spirituality, seeing it as a private matter.

- They clarified the difference between right and wrong.

- God was impersonal.

Paul and Joann then listed the emotional and social legacies they received from their parents. As they lined them up, two things became clear. Paul had received the stronger emotional legacy. His "stabilizer bar" was in much better shape than Joann's. Second, their social legacies were mixed, similar to their spiritual legacies. The husband and wife had good relational elements in each legacy, but neither was perfect. They had a fairly solid foundation, but some issues would need to be addressed.

Our Emotional Legacy

Paul's	*Joann's*
• Home was a safe environment.	• Home was an unsafe environment.
• Home was financially stable.	• Home was financially stable.
• I developed positive identity and self-worth.	• I developed a positive identity, but weak self-worth.
• My parents created an emotional resting place.	• No emotional resting place created. The opposite was true: It was a very angry family.
• You could measure up if you could perform.	• No matter how you performed, you couldn't measure up.

Our Social Legacy

Paul's	*Joann's*
• Clear borders were established.	• Clear borders were established.
• I was taught to respect others.	• I was taught to respect others.
• I had been given responsibility and trusted to carry it out.	• I was taught responsibility and given opportunity to prove myself.

Paul's	*Joann's*
• Parents dictatorially enforced rules—not in context of a loving relationship.	• Parents dictatorially enforced rules.
• Communication was taught, although sometimes a forced communication.	• I was taught to communicate, although sometimes our conversations were forced.

After listing the major areas of concern, we outlined the heritage they wanted to give. We identified what to keep, what to throw out, and what to enhance. For instance, under their emotional legacies they recognized that upon marriage they had not intentionally kept his good elements and discarded her bad ones. Here was a clear opportunity for them to move in a positive direction. As we discussed strategies, Paul and Joann saw how a new heritage could rise out of the ashes of the old. A spark of hope entered the room.

2. CHOOSING WHAT TO KEEP

The second step in creating a single, united heritage plan is to determine those aspects of your heritage you want to keep. This is a sorting process that will lead to a new list, one that will feature aspects from your three legacy lists and those of your spouse.

Here are the lists that Paul and Joann developed in each of the three legacy dimensions. Rather than reject every item from their own heritage in favor of their spouse's, the couple defined what elements of their combined heritage should be kept. (The strengths of each partner for specific items are shown in parentheses. The partner acknowledged his or her strengths and weaknesses.)

Spiritual Legacy

Unseen spiritual realities were recognized. (Paul stronger)
Spirituality is important. (Both weak)
Involvement in spiritual things is vital. (Both weak)
Right and wrong need to be clearly defined. (Both strong)
God is a personal God. (Paul stronger)

Emotional Legacy

Create a safe environment. (Paul stronger)
Create financial stability. (Both strong)
Create an emotional resting place. (Paul stronger)
Create positive identity and self-worth. (Paul stronger)

Social Legacy

Clear borders need to be established. (Both strong)
Responsibilities need to be given—and trust to be carried out. (Both strong)
Teach communication. (Joann stronger)

3. *CHOOSING WHAT TO REPLACE*

The next step is to answer the question, "What aspects of your combined heritage should be replaced?" As your spouse and you do that, you are able to identify problem areas in your heritage. Paul and Joann were able to recognize several issues:

Spiritual Legacy

- We must replace our vision of unseen realities as hypocritical, superficial, and impersonal with a strong acknowledgment and daily reinforcement of spiritual realities.

- We must toss out the idea that spirituality was something for social protocol—to be seen but not necessarily adhered to. We will replace it with a desire to make spiritual activities a vital and intricate part of every aspect of life. We want our practice to be regular, not sporadic.

- We must replace private spiritual issues with an open and transparent conversation that would reinforce spiritual commitments.

- We must replace an impersonal God with a God who is a personal close friend, who cares deeply about the everyday efforts of our life.

Emotional Legacy

- We will work to increase Joann's self-worth, while keeping the positive identity and self-worth of Paul.

- We will replace ruling by anger and help prepare an emotional resting place for Joann's children. (The counselor helped Joann to understand the nature of an emotional resting place.)

- So that deep emotional roots can grow, we will replace a performance-based acceptance and institute an "it's not what you do, but who you are" type relationship for the children (especially Joann's, who are more affected at present).

Since both Paul and Joann were given a generally healthy relational legacy, this area was not as critical, except for one component. We tossed out an angry, dictatorial, and confrontational type of communication and inserted a balanced love with behavioral borders. It was then they could begin to model clear and sensitive communication skills.

After working with Paul and Joann to identify how they might blend their mixed heritage into one, they were able to begin building a plan for moving forward. They were no longer victims of an unclear mix of ingredients, some healthy, others not. Instead, they had established a clear goal for what they wanted their mixed heritage to become. The hard work is just beginning, but the hope of new beginnings and the synergy of mutual commitment has launched them in the right direction.

Paul and Joann are making great progress creating a better heritage than they ever thought possible. It is a daily battle, but they refuse to give up. I am optimistic that they will be successful. More important, so are they.

THE TOUGH CASES

The process of creating a mixed heritage is going to be harder for some parents than others. Two people who are from similar backgrounds with no prior marriages will have an easier time than two people who were previously divorced with children and who have dramatically different religious, ethnic, and cultural histories. There are countless variables that make the process more complex for family B than for family A. But there are three types of families that face great challenges in creating a healthy, positive mixed heritage: divorced single parents, those from differing cultures, and blended families. Here are some cautions and suggestions for those parents.

DIVORCED SINGLE PARENTS

The job of single parenting is hard work, requiring tireless, selfless effort. Those who are single parents due to the death of a spouse or abandonment by a biological father or mother face a tremendous burden trying to build a solid heritage alone. But divorced single parents often have an especially difficult time when the other parent is still involved with the kids.

Janet is divorced because her husband, a former minister, "fell in love" with another woman and considered the pleasure of sin more compelling than the responsibility of faithfulness. She works hard to support two young sons on her own, with no financial help from their dad. The courts mandated that she must allow the boys to spend time with their father, so she cooperates. But it is difficult to watch them spend time on weekends with "Disneyland

Daddy"—a father who showers them with treats or trips to shows and other amusements—especially since another woman is now in his bed.

"I try to teach my boys right and wrong," an exhausted Janet shares. "I bring them to church and sacrifice to put them through a Christian school. I don't have the money or energy for either, but I know they need the influence of others who believe as I do. To be painfully honest, though, I face a daily temptation to throw in the towel and escape from reality. I hold on and keep going for one reason—I don't want my boys to get a totally bad heritage just because their father is irresponsible."

Like most single parents, the mixed messages the children receive from Mom and Dad make Janet's job much more difficult. She only controls one-half of the boys' mixed heritage, and the other half is anything but healthy. What is a divorced single parent to do?

First, whatever you do, don't give up! Half a positive heritage is far better than none at all. There are countless examples of kids from similar circumstances who mature into well-adjusted, solid adults thanks exclusively to the diligent efforts of a faithful, selfless single parent.

Second, seek out those who may be willing to give an extended heritage. Expose your kids to intact traditional families on a regular basis to show them what can be. At the same time, don't allow anyone to make them feel ashamed of you or their own heritage. Giving them a model of what is best should, in no way, imply that their own situation is hopeless. Single-parent families are still families!

Finally, if at all possible, come to some kind of agreement with your ex-mate. For the sake of the kids, try to discuss how the influence of each parent can be blended . . . even with separation and the feelings associated of past hurt. Obviously, many divorced couples will find this step extremely difficult, if not impossible. But try, for the sake of those kids you both love.

Be encouraged. Your task is difficult, but many have done it well. So can you!

PARENTS FROM DIFFERENT
CULTURES, RACES, OR RELIGIONS

Paul, a black man, is married to Kathy, a white woman. They share the same religious faith, the same tastes in music and movies, and the same appetite for spicy foods. But they don't share the same skin color. And members of both races don't like that fact—which comes across through the subtle, yet clear comments of disapproval.

"Have you considered how hard it will be for your children—being racially mixed and all?" or "Do you think society is ready to accept this? I mean, many people are still very prejudiced." More often than not, the comments represent veiled criticism rather than sincere concern.

Bob was born and raised in "good ol' America" with Mom, apple pie, and Chevrolet. His wife, Ingrid, grew up on the other side of the ocean with her *frau*, apple strudel, and Volvo. The two met while he was stationed in Germany with the army. They love each other deeply. But they frequently encounter differing assumptions, preferences, and expectations as they try to mix their cultural backgrounds.

Kevin grew up in a very traditional Presbyterian church where liturgy and organ music were part of each and every worship service. Joy, his wife, was raised in a hand-clappin,' Amen-shoutin,' Southern Baptist fellowship. Guess what aspect of their life causes conflict?

All of these couples face the added complexity of differing cultural and ethnic backgrounds as they seek to create a mixed heritage for their children. Often they have different values and expectations. In addition, they may face social and cultural biases as they interact with other parents. Each must create a single heritage for their children . . . against the odds.

As our melting pot society produces more interracial, intercultural, and interfaith marriages, we will need to become more experienced at the process of making the blend work. In the meantime, however, such families face unique struggles. We offer a few tips.

First, don't sweat the small stuff. There are millions of tiny issues any couple could "nitpick" if they wanted to do so. But most of them really don't matter. Every family must learn the art of compromise if it hopes to survive. At times, it may be necessary to swallow your pride and back down; you may need to give in more often than you'd like. Do it! A bit of humility never hurt anyone.

Second, don't make a mountain out of a molehill. Resist the temptation to view your situation as worse than everyone else's. Don't wear a chip on your shoulder just because you think everyone disapproves of your interracial marriage. Everyone doesn't. Don't feel sorry for yourself because your wife cooks exotic dishes, unlike mother's meat and potato meals. At least you're eating! Don't abandon church just because you can't agree on one that meets 100 percent of both your expectations. There is no such church. In short, don't act like you are so different from other families. You aren't.

Third, remember the goal. Your objective is not to pass a heritage that is identical to the one you were given. It is rather to blend the best from each into a single inheritance of love. Doing that requires a selfless attitude on the part of both husband and wife—especially when the differences are extreme.

THE BLENDED FAMILY

The blended family has much more of a chance to collapse than a family unit with the original parents. The blended families I counsel have pointed out the four major areas of brittleness, the stress points where cracks are likely to occur, where turbulence may cause a vibration to shake the household into a possible collapse.

The first stress point is discipline. Husband and wife discover quickly that resentment builds up when the stepparent tries to discipline the other's birth child. "You aren't that strict with yours. . . . You spank mine harder. . . . You seem to enjoy it when you discipline my child and hate it when you discipline yours. . . . I will not tolerate your child speaking to me in that manner." Sometimes one parent accuses the other of favoritism: "If you do that for yours, do it for mine too. . . . You spend more time with yours than you do with mine." And the children often pick up the drumbeat, assailing the stepparent's right to discipline, "What gives you the right to order me around? You're not my real daddy!" Emotions run very high on this issue.

My advice on this problem is to neutralize it entirely. How? Agree that whenever possible, the birth parent will carry out any necessary discipline on his or her own child—not the stepparent. Appropriate discipline rarely needs to be administered quickly, leaving plenty of time for the issue to be addressed with the birth parent for proper handling. Efficient? Perhaps not. But it is much more effective. The risk of resentment and perceived inconsistency is too high to handle it any other way.

The second stress point is the ex-husband or ex-wife. Usually his or her entrance into the picture is with some sort of demand. More often than not, his routine, discipline, and perhaps even values do not line up with yours. After the children spend a weekend at the ex's, it is often necessary to go back to ground zero and reestablish the right angle.

One way to give your child some sure footing amid this "tug-of-war" is to create what I call a "behavioral contract." This tool is useful for any family, but it has been particularly helpful with the blended families I've counseled. Here's how it works: Clearly establish the behavioral guidelines for your household, and outline them in a contract document. Set forth clear "minimum behavioral standards" for everyone in your home—such as honesty, respect, and cleanliness—which the child will be expected to meet. Then go the next step by attaching a different set of privileges to different behavior standards. For example, you may attach frequent car access privileges to a teenage son to his respecting an early curfew. As long as he agrees to and abides by the curfew guideline, the car privilege is given. Or for your daughter you may attach an increased wardrobe budget to completing certain household chores. Again, if the behavior is on target, the accompanying benefits should be given.

In establishing a contract, build a sense of joint ownership by allowing the child to select from among several contracts you've drafted. Or better yet, seek the child's input into his or her own contract creation. This contract becomes a clear, mutually agreed upon standard of behavior for that child—whether he or she is in your house or with the other parent. Most important, it provides a forum for dialogue on what is and is not appropriate behavior within your household.

The third stress point for the blended family is overcurious and overstimulated teens from different families. A stepbrother and stepsister combination can be fertile ground for moral temptation, even abuse. I've counseled several women who endured sexual abuse by an older stepbrother in the home. Sadly, it's a quite common occurrence with blended families. But it can occur both ways. I'll never forget a counseling session I had several years ago with a young man I'll call Joe. He revealed that when he was seven years old an older stepsister began sexually molesting him. "I never told anyone because I didn't think they would believe me," Joe shared years after the abuse. "After all, how often do you hear about a girl abusing a boy?" Unfortunately, it happens more often than we'd like to think.

My advice—be aware! Don't assume your kids are immune to this temptation. I don't recommend paranoia. But I strongly suggest that you be alert to what can and does happen among stepsiblings, take the appropriate precautions, and establish "just in case" safeguards.

The fourth stress point is the inevitable conflicts over where the kids will spend the holidays. Because so many family members are involved as well as relatives and step-relatives and because of sheer logistics, holidays can be a nightmare. These times of the year can be earth-shattering. Mixing all the necessary ingredients correctly can make the resulting product less than tasteful, if not just plain hard and not easily swallowed.

This final problem area has a simple solution: plan ahead. If your kids must spend Thanksgiving or Christmas with your ex, celebrate your own holiday together early. Do your best to arrange annual vacations when the kids are with you. Remember, those special times together are an important part of your heritage-building process. Plan well in advance so that you, and the kids, don't miss out.

If not closely watched, things can get out of balance. When that happens, you may despair of ever passing on a strong heritage; you want only to survive. As one exasperated couple told me, "We actually wanted to just run away . . . we found ourselves actually wishing our lives and our children's lives away!"

You may find yourself in the same emotional boat. I'll tell you what I tell Paul and Joann. "Don't give up! Yes, the battle is tough. *This is your Normandy.* But your efforts to give your kids a positive heritage, even against the odds, will be worth it in the long run. Remember, someone has to pay the price in order to break the cycle."

WINNING THE TOUGH CASES

I am counseling through the blending process several families who fall into one or more of these tough scenarios. We are trying to create a successful heritage to pass on to their children. Their success, so far, lies in creating a right angle that everyone in the house understands and lives by. The plumb line is straight and true, not by chance, but by planned efforts of caring parents. The parents often memorize the "Leading Legacy Indicators," and they establish checkpoints along the breadth of each child's experiences. Mom and Dad show a united front and are determined to fight their own "Normandy" if necessary.

Have they been successful? Well, we haven't come to the conclusion yet; their children are still growing, making mistakes and learning (so are the parents, for that matter). I guess the proof of the pudding will be in the eating. At this point, we are just sampling . . . but the taste, so far, is delightful.

Chapter Fourteen

PLANNING YOUR HERITAGE

L et's face it. The chief reason many of us fail to give a solid heritage is not lack of desire, incompetence, or even the baggage from our past. The number one reason we fail to give a solid heritage is negligence—we neglect to create a plan for doing so. The typical family reacts to the daily events of life, instead of intentionally planning the heritage-passing process. So they find themselves ricocheting through daily family life, bouncing here and there.

Big mistake!

As the Japanese proverb puts it, "When you're dying of thirst it's too late to think about digging a well." Sadly, many parents don't even think about the impact of their heritage process until it is too late. I know, because many of them end up in my office seeking crisis intervention for their children.

The chief reason we wrote this book is that we believe anyone can give a strong heritage. But doing so requires a plan. Everything you've read so far has been preparation for this chapter.

By now you more fully understand the heritage. Great! Understanding is important. But creating a heritage plan is the key to making it happen. I urge you to complete the heritage-planning process contained on these pages. It is designed to help you begin the process of weaving the heritage cord for your children.

You will walk through several vital steps in the heritage-planning process, some of which will be review from earlier exercises. You will be asked to: (1) summarize the strong and weak elements of the heritage you were given, (2) identify to whom you seek to give a heritage, (3) state your goal—writing a description of the heritage you hope to give, (4) seek the Lord's help and wisdom as you begin what may be new to you and to those you love, and (5) learn how to use the tool chest by incorporating the family fragrance, impression points, the right angle, and tradition into your heritage.

After you complete this process, you will create a "heritage calendar" in which you will list specific principles, activities, and events on specific days of the week, month, and year.

Of course, once the plan is created, it must be carried out. But experience tells us that those who write down a plan are much more likely to get it done. So, let's not delay another minute. Roll up your sleeves and start creating the game plan.

WHAT YOU RECEIVED

This step is designed to highlight the good and bad of your own heritage. This will help you choose what kind of hand-me-downs you and your loved ones will wear. Review the evaluation you completed in your "Personal Heritage Survey," pages 95–97. That survey includes your ratings of your spiritual, emotional, and social legacies and a summary of your leading legacy indicators.

On a piece of paper or by photocopying, make a copy of items 1 and 2 of the "Personal Heritage Survey." This summary of your heritage is the foundation of your plan.

WHO WILL RECEIVE FROM YOU

Identify the people in your life to whom you wish to give a heritage. If you are married with children, the priority is obvious. But the extended heritage is also a vital part of what you give, especially if you are single, childless, or beyond the child-rearing years. For example, you may identify Sally, that little girl in your Sunday school class at church. Or perhaps Chuck, the child of a single mom, who needs a strong male role model in his life.

To whom do you seek to give a strong heritage? List their names below:

Family members:

_____   _____

_____   _____

_____   _____

Others:

_____   _____

_____   _____

WHAT YOU WANT TO GIVE

Now set your goal. What do you want to give? You may wish to return to the exercise "Designing Your Heritage," pages 98–99, considering again the items you want to keep (K) or strengthen (S). You may want to add to the list or change any specifics in light of what you've read since. As you draft your goal, ask yourself this question: "When those I love reflect upon the heritage they were given, what do I want them to remember?" Use these spaces to record your goals.

The Spiritual Legacy I/we want to give:

_____

_____

_____

_____

_____

_____

The Emotional Legacy I/we want to give:

_____

_____

_____

_____

_____

The Social Legacy I/we want to give:

_____

_____

_____

_____

_____

SEEKING HELP

Before you go any farther, take some time to seek help. Go before the Lord and admit your weaknesses with regard to the heritage process. Confess where you've failed, and ask for help as you seek to make a fresh start. Ask Him to give you the wisdom and strength needed to break the cycle and give what you didn't get. You may even need to ask Him to inject the desire into your soul, enabling you to overcome a selfish or apathetic attitude. He will come alongside you as you begin the heritage-building process, if you ask Him. Use the space below to write a prayer of commitment and petition for wisdom before you begin building your detailed plan.

Dear Lord:

_____

_____

_____

_____

_____

A second source of help is other people. There are others around you who have passed along, or are now passing, a solid heritage. Spend time with them. Learn from them. Ask questions. Steal ideas! However you do it, try to benefit from the input and example of those who are doing it well. Remember, iron sharpens iron.

Think of two to four individuals who may be a source of help along the way. Then meet with them, asking them to serve as your "Heritage Consultants." Most people would be glad to share ideas, tips, and advice.

USING THE HERITAGE TOOL CHEST

The most powerful means for passing a solid heritage is to proactively use the tools described in chapters 7 through 10. Although you can apply them in whatever way works best for your family, we recommend different applications for each of the four tools.

FREQUENCY

Family Fragrance. The goal of the family fragrance (chapter 7) is to create an ongoing environment of love in the home.

So we recommend that you identify *daily* activities and patterns in the home which create a sweet-smelling aroma.

Impression Points. Impression points (chapter 8) are used to intentionally and incidentally impress your values upon others. And while incidental impression points will occur any time, we recommend intentionally creating at least one impression point on a *weekly* basis.

Right Angle. Setting the right angle (chapter 9) involves instilling a sense of what is normal, healthy living into the hearts and minds of those we love. While it is imperative that we model these principles on a consistent basis, it is helpful to develop a plan for emphasizing each on a *monthly* basis. In other words, once you've identified your list of right-angle principles, plan to focus on one every month throughout the year.

Tradition. Traditions (chapter 10) are created in order to instill a strong sense of identity. Because they are generally attached to some memorable event or holiday, they tend to be set on an *annual* basis. During these annual traditions we make a special effort to reinforce the family formula, retell the family stories, and highlight the important aspects of your family identity.

SPECIFIC PLANS

Now for the fun part. Put on your creative thinking cap and begin identifying the specific things you plan to do in order to make your heritage goal a reality over the next twelve-month period. Go back to the "Getting Personal" sections of chapters 7 through 10, and grab the ideas you drafted there. You may also wish to prime the creative pump by scanning the suggestions listed in the appendix, beginning on page 257. Whether you borrow or create your own specifics, write them down in the spaces provided below or in a notebook.

Family Fragrance

How I plan to create an environment of love in my home.

Planning Your Heritage

Every day I will demonstrate affection *by* . . .

_____

_____

_____

Every day I will assure respect *for the individual by* . . .

_____

_____

_____

Every day I will create a sense of order *by* . . .

_____

_____

_____

Every day I will foster merriment *by* . . .

_____

_____

_____

Every day I will give affirmation *by* . . .

_____

_____

_____

Impression Points

How I plan to intentionally impress my values upon those I love.

243

Every week, I will create impression points by . . .

What _____

(List activity)

When _____

(Day & time of the week)

How _____

_____

(Describe specifics and what needs to be done in advance)

What _____

(List activity)

When _____

(Day & time of the week)

How _____

_____

(Describe specifics and what needs to be done in advance)

Right Angle

How I plan to model and instill a healthy sense of "normal" for my family.

Below are blanks to develop month-by-month principles that you want to be part of the right angle that drops a straight plumb of standards for your children. To better establish the right angle each month, consider incorporating the monthly principles into your weekly impression point activities. In other words, use the impression point "hammer" to drive your right angle "nails."

Each month, I plan to emphasize a different right angle principle by . . .

Planning Your Heritage

January Principle: _____
I plan to emphasize it by . . .

_____

_____

February Principle: _____
I plan to emphasize it by . . .

_____

_____

March Principle: _____
I plan to emphasize it by . . .

_____

_____

April Principle: _____
I plan to emphasize it by . . .

_____

_____

May Principle: _____
I plan to emphasize it by . . .

_____

_____

June Principle: _____
I plan to emphasize it by . . .

_____

_____

July Principle: _____
I plan to emphasize it by . . .

_____

_____

August Principle: _____
I plan to emphasize it by . . .

_____

_____

September Principle: _____
I plan to emphasize it by . . :

_____

_____

October Principle: _____
I plan to emphasize it by . . .

_____

_____

November Principle: _____
I plan to emphasize it by . . .

_____

_____

December Principle: _____
I plan to emphasize it by . . .

_____

_____

Traditions

Remember, family traditions reinforce a child's sense of personal and family identity. They are useful in developing a family creed, the belief system by which you want your children to live. In this section you will write out your creed and then list events that can become traditions to reinforce that creed and your child's identity.

The Family Creed

I will use family traditions to reinforce our family formula, which can be summarized as follows (review page 183, where you wrote the first draft of your creed):

We believe . . .

_____

_____

_____

_____

Events

Below is the first month of a list you can prepare of events that can establish family traditions.

At a minimum, I plan to celebrate each of the following events in our home, making each a special and meaningful part of our family traditions.

January: (New Year's Day, Super Bowl party)

Event _____
(List occasion)

When _____
(Day of month)

247

How _____

_____

(Describe specifics and what needs to be done in preparation)

Event _____

(List occasion)

When _____

(Day of month)

How _____

_____

(Describe specifics and what needs to be done in preparation)

Now, on a piece of paper, prepare a monthly listing of likely events, beginning with February. Use the January listing of *event, when,* and *how* above as your pattern. Try to create two events each month. Be sure to invite your spouse-to-be in on the planning. Consider asking one or more of your children to join in as well; they can be creative and will have a sense of ownership on those activities they suggested.

Obviously, birthdays and other such personal events should be included in the appropriate month. To help you along, here is a list of seasonal events and suggested events for each month. But be sure to come up with many of your own as well.

February. Groundhog Day, Valentine's Day, "I can't stand another day of winter" Day, Presidents' Day. *March:* St. Patrick's Day, first day of spring, Clean the Garage Day. *April:* Passion Week, Passover, and Easter. *May:* Mother's Day, Memorial Day, Mow the Grass Day. *June:* Father's Day, first day of summer, Flag Day, School's Out Day. *July:* Independence Day, Backyard Tent Sleepover, Camping Trip. *August:* "Random acts of love" Day, Family Baseball Series, End of Summer party. *September:* Labor

Day, first day of fall, Rosh Hashanah, New Friend Day. *October:* Yom Kippur, Reformation Day, Halloween. *November:* Thanksgiving, Family Game Showdown, Veterans Day. *December:* Hannukah, Christmas, Post Holiday "Beat the blues" Day.

STORIES

In chapter 10 (page 184) you wrote down one story you could tell from the life of your family. Now let's add other stories you can tell as part of the traditions.

I plan to share the following stories with my family, drawn from our lives and the lives of past generations, in order to give my family a strong sense of connection to the past and to one another.

_____

_____

_____

_____

_____

CREATE YOUR HERITAGE CALENDAR

Once you've completed the creative steps, it is time to transfer your wonderful ideas onto a calendar. If the goals, concepts, and activities you've identified don't find their way onto the everyday calendar you use to run family affairs, they will not happen. Again, good intentions won't get it done. But specific activities on the calendar, with a plan of action behind them, will put you on the road toward creating and giving an inheritance of love.

As we stated early in the book, there is nothing mystical or necessarily profound about creating a strong heritage. It is a discipline, not a gift. Creating a heritage calendar is a vital step along the path of making the goal a reality and turning "someday" into "today."

A FINAL THOUGHT

For many, the most difficult part of passing a solid legacy is the creative process. Many ask themselves, "Where do I get the ideas?" We have found that there are countless sources of great ideas for passing a strong heritage. Every day, millions of families engage in activities that fall into one of our four categories: family fragrance, impression points, the right angle, or traditions.

In order to bring the ideas and the people together, we've launched the Heritage Builders Association. Our efforts include a periodic newsletter which draws upon that wealth of heritage creativity—average families. Our goal is to provide a forum through which families can share success stories and tips, allowing families to indirectly contribute to one another's heritage process. And the best part is that these ideas have been created and tested in the laboratory of the home.

If you would like to participate in this cooperative effort by becoming part of the Heritage Builders Association, send $15 for annual membership dues to:

HERITAGE BUILDERS ASSOCIATION
P.O. Box 62254
Colorado Springs, CO 80962
E-mail: Hbuilders@aol.com

Epilogue

BONE-WEARY
JOY

Adam and Renee seemed to have everything. They had good employment; they owned several houses. Their daughter was healthy and pretty. Their church family loved them. They were involved in civic affairs in their east Texas town.

As their daughter, Jody, grew through her elementary years, everything was rosy. When she entered adolescence, things began to slowly change. Jody began to unfold her wings to stretch. Mostly, she moved in the wrong direction. Adam and Renee would confront her. But they had no clear right angle . . . no clear instructions had been defined.

The parents sought and received good counsel, but they chose to ignore it because it required consistent effort and sacrifice on their part. *We work hard enough just earning a living,* they reasoned. They just didn't want to deal with it.

Jody progressively became worse. She began to smoke and made friends with kids who had taken drugs.

"Oh, she will be all right," Renee tried to reassure herself and Adam. "We turned out OK . . . didn't we?"

The downward spiral continued. Arguments. Flying verbal spears. Physical encounters. Dad began to be absent, avoiding the problem with overtime. Lots of overtime. Finally, he took a job in Saudi Arabia, where he had to live for a year before the family could join him. He just wanted relief.

Jody kept going backward. The absence of Dad added to the problem. The pressure built until Renee finally took the easy road and said, "Do whatever you want. It's your own life to ruin."

Renee consoled herself by sleeping excessive and unusual hours. That sleep addiction created an ever-widening rift between her and Adam . . . they both felt guilty . . . yet blamed each other.

Eventually, Renee and other family members found themselves at Jody's hospital bed. A bullet from a gang shooting now lodged in Jody's head.

Paradise to devastation. Two crushed hearts. Sobbing, sobbing, and more sobbing.

HERITAGE KILLERS

Jody was a victim of her own choices. Her parents cannot be blamed for the lifestyle she entered. But things might have been different . . . if only. If only Adam and Renee had started earlier. If only they had made their daughter's life a higher priority than a nice house, a new car, or a big promotion. If only they would have regarded the effort and tension in dealing with their daughter's struggle as worth the hard work. If only they had heeded the counsel they were given. If only . . .

Adam and Renee fell victim to all of the most common heritage killers. They stepped right into those destructive traps which rob families of the ability to give a positive heritage. The tears of heartache are the legacy of their error.

As you now begin to develop a heritage for your children, be aware of the most common heritage killers, those attitudes and actions that can undermine a growing legacy. Here are the three most common heritage killers: selfishness, busyness, and reactive living. Let's examine each of them.

1. SELFISHNESS

Nothing will kill a heritage faster than selfishness. When we become consumed with self, it is impossible to be concerned with others. The process of building and giving a solid legacy requires an ongoing, tireless commitment to the future well-being of those we love, rather than a preoccupation with our own comfort and satisfaction. The remedy? Replace selfish living with selfless giving. Take your eyes off of "me, myself, and I" and place them on those around you who need what only you can give.

2. BUSYNESS

Letting a busy schedule dominate our lives is also a heritage-killer. In fact, it is second only to selfishness in distancing parents from their kids, both in terms of knowing the children and having their respect. If we don't spend much time with our children, how can we know them?

Planning, preparing, and then passing along a solid heritage requires time. When a majority of our time is committed to this and that meeting, project, or personal activity, we will be giving leftover time (and little of it) to our children. The remedy? Keep first things first. Be sure to protect the time needed for family in the midst of the daily scurry. Certainly, many important things need to be done. But what could be more important than giving your family the heritage they deserve?

3. REACTIVE LIVING

Reactive living means responding passively to circumstances, rather than proactively driving them. It's one life at a time, without planning ahead and having a goal. There is nothing noble about letting life happen. We must take the heritage process by the reins and steer it in the right direction.

Reactive living can kill a heritage by not planning for it, letting events and circumstances override our intentions for the family. What's the remedy? As we've emphasized over and over, create a plan of how, when, and where you will make your heritage goals a reality. It won't just happen—it must be done!

WHEN WILL YOU CRY?

Clearly it's easy to undermine a growing heritage. The last thing we want to do in this book is give the mistaken impression that building, handling, and passing a heritage is a walk in the park. But it is rewarding, as we have seen.

It also is tiring and painful.

The principles may be simple, but the task is by no means easy. It requires lots of time and energy. It allows little rest. There will be frequent periods when you will be tired—bone tired!

As I watch Renee wipe a tear from her cheek, my mind goes back to those times when my own children were in bed, already down for the night. I would awake at one o'clock in the morning to the sight of my wife, Gail, finalizing some of the heritage-passing chores she needed to get done. I'd call her to bed, knowing that her wake-up call was only a few hours away. It was during those times she had to let go. Tears came. They could not be stopped. They were neither tears of sorrow nor joy. They were not the tears of a whiner, nor of a "poor ol' me" attitude. They were tears of pure exhaustion. Hers was a heavy load, because she was a working mom who insisted on making the heritage process a priority.

A sweet-smelling family fragrance does not just happen. Establishing a solid right angle takes diligent effort. Intentional impression points must be planned and prepared for if they are going to occur. Family traditions require long hours of loving labor. Gail knew the price. But she also knew the ultimate payoff.

Renee reveals her heartache. "I wish I had taken the time. I wish I would have expended the energy. I wish I could do it again."

Both Gail and Renee have a legacy of tears. For Renee they are tears of sorrow, tears of loss, tears of regret. For Gail, they are tears of exhaustion, tears of selfless giving, tears of a job well done. Gail's tears came early, while she dealt with the setbacks of planning the heritage; Renee's came later, the outcome of not planning and expending energy on the heritage. Our question to you is this: When will you cry?

Never forget, there is hope. You can stop the bad generational flow and establish a new, wonderful heritage for those you love. It is our desire that what you have read will give you reason to finish the job. The task may weary you at times, but the effort is worth it.

Someday you may regret that you didn't make more money, or that you didn't see the world, but you will never regret the bone-weary time you gave to carry, and pass on, that good heritage. Joy awaits at the end, when you hand off the baton to your now-adult children.

On behalf of future generations, we thank you for taking time to create and give the heritage.

Appendix

PRIMING
THE PUMP

To get the creative juices going, we've listed a few ideas that can strengthen one or more of our four tools in the heritage chest: family fragrance, impression points, right angle, and tradition. These suggestions have been tested in the heritage-passing laboratory in real homes of average families like your own. Feel free to steal shamelessly from this list or any other source of good ideas you can find. Remember, the key to success is not originality, but action.

FAMILY NIGHTS

Jim's kids are all standing at the foot of the stairs. Dad is at the top of that same staircase. They wait eagerly for instructions. Tonight is "Family Night" at the Weidmann home—a weekly ritual in which Dad spends time intentionally impressing his values upon the family. "Here is the assignment. I'll take everyone to Baskin Robbins who is able to get to where I am from down there." He has the attention of all four kids. "But there are a few rules. First, you can't touch the stairs. Second, you can't touch the railing. Now, begin!"

After several contemplative moments, the youngest speaks up. "That's impossible, Dad! How can we get to where you are without touching the stairs or the railing?" After some disgruntled agreement from two of the other children, the oldest gets an idea. "Hey, Dad. Come down here." Jim walks down the stairs. "Now bend over while I get on your back. OK, climb the stairs."

Of course, the plan works. Jim proceeds to parallel the solution to this game with how it is impossible to get to God on our own. "When we let God do the work on our behalf, we can get to heaven," Jim explains. After a trip up the stairs on Dad's back, the whole gang piles into the minivan for a double scoop of mint chocolate chip.

Family Night is a method being used in more and more homes and is one of the best concepts we've encountered for successfully impressing values on kids. If you would like to learn more about how to create Family Nights in your home, request the introductiory "Impressions" series when you write to the Heritage Builders Association.[1] (See page 250 for our address.)

GOOD NIGHT, GOOD MORNING

Areas of conflict with the kids in most homes happen in two time slots—when it is time to put the kids in bed, and when it is time to get them out of bed. My style was to holler to the kids, "You kids better get in that bed—or I'm going to jail for homicide!" In the Ledbetter home, I tried to get them up in the morning with sensory overload: flash the overhead light on and off, sing loudly and off-key, and irritate them right out of bed and into a lousy mood. I'd deal with the lousy mood later or, once they were up, leave for work. Gail decided maybe it would be better if she came up with a more composed way.

For bedtime, she piled into one of the children's beds and read books to them. She also purchased beautifully produced cassette recordings of stories, letting the children play them only at 8 P.M. As a result, the children began to look forward to their bedtime. The evening calm returned to our house.

In the mornings, she entered their rooms quietly with a cup of hot chocolate or juice and sweet rolls placed beside their beds. She would turn their cassettes over to play them again. Sometimes she sat quietly on the edge of their beds and rubbed them awake, greeted them with a smile, and welcomed them to a new morning. She started and ended each day by creating a calm sense of order.

You can invent your own "Good Night, Good Morning" ritual. You may not choose to offer a beverage with sweet rolls, but with a little creativity, you can make your children want to get up—and, at night, go to bed.

SIGN ON THE DOTTED LINE

No element of the heritage is more important than the spiritual legacy. One way to solidify a decision for Christ is to drive a stake in time, a marker that your child can look back on and realize his commitment to God is real. It is like the pile of stones the Israelites left in the Jordan River upon crossing into the Promised Land (Joshua 3:9–4:9). One way to create such a marker is to draw up a "contract" between your child and you. Though not legally binding, of course, it gives your child a point in time to remind him or her of the personal decision to follow Christ.

The wording may vary from the one below, which is only a sample. Importantly, it reflects your child's spiritual knowledge and needs at the time it is signed. Stan drafted the following contract when his son Eddie was age eight; it still hangs signed on the wall today—a reminder of their mutual agreement. It reads like this:

> We, the undersigned, on this 25th day of December, 1991, do hereby agree to live our lives in obedience to God's Word, the Bible, and to keep Jesus Christ as the Lord of our lives.
>
> In doing so, "Party A," the father, gives assurance to "Party B," the son (or daughter), that he (or she) will be in heaven, so as to have an eternity to spend together. As did

"Party A," "Party B"gives assurance to "Party A" that he will be in heaven, making the eternal relationship possible.

Both parties recognize that entrance into heaven is not the result of their works, but rather by the Grace of God, through the death of Jesus Christ on the Cross. We also trust the Holy Spirit for His help in meeting the terms of this contract, as well as the promises of Scripture.

It is this saving work of the Lord Jesus Christ, that gives the undersigned the confidence to enter into this agreement. With men, it would be impossible, but with God, All Things Are Possible!

Signed This Day, Before Jehovah God:

_____   _____
Stanley R. John (aka: Daddy)   Date

_____   _____
Eddie John (aka: Son)   Date

Eddie will never forget the importance of his decision to follow Christ thanks to Dad's effort to create this wonderful impression point.

LONG-DISTANCE GRANDMA

One creative way to pass along a heritage to a distant relative is via tape recordings and books. If you have grandchildren or nieces/nephews you want to influence with a strong heritage, but can't be with them regularly, consider the power of audio and visual gifts that contain the right messages.

Yvette and her husband live eight hundred miles away from their nearest relatives, including Yvette's parents. But Yvette's mother found a way to influence her young grandchildren. Every now and then, Grandma sends the children new books to be read at bedtime. Along with the books comes a cassette tape. The tape has Grandma's voice reading the books, including an occasional question or comment to the kids—"Isn't that Mr. Rabbit silly?" or "What do you think he's going to do next?" Mom or Dad grab a book, sit the kids on their lap, start the tape, and let Grandma make an impression point.

CELEBRATING PURITY

Thirteen-year-old Rachel plans to remain sexually pure until her wedding night. She made a formal commitment to that goal at the start of puberty one year ago. To mark her commitment, Rachel's parents arranged a special ceremony for her which they called "A Celebration of Purity."

The family dressed up, gathered for a formal banquet, with the menu and program printed and placed on each plate. The order of celebration included Dinner (featuring Mama), Ceremony (featuring Papa, Mama, Grandpa and Grandma, and close family friends), Special Music, Signing of the Purity Covenant Certificate, and Presentation of a Covenant Gift.

With the exception of her actual wedding ceremony, nothing will make a greater impression on Rachel of the beauty and purity of God's design for sexuality. Parents can create memorable moments for their teenage children through such pledges, and they can be handled a variety of ways.[2] If you choose to include a purity covenant, ask your daughter or son to help in writing the actual sentences of the first draft. Let your child have ownership in the covenant.

LIVING ROOM PICNIC

The kids are restless. It's bitter cold outside and the snow is falling—a perfect time for a family picnic! Grab a big blanket, throw it down on the living room floor, bring out the sandwiches and chips, and enjoy a picnic in front of the fireplace. Such off-the-wall, spur-of-the-moment activities quickly turn into family traditions that can spark all kinds of family fun.

HOLIDAY CARING

Every year during Christmas week, the Brown family shops for presents, prepares delicious food, jumps in the car, and heads off to carry out an annual ritual of love. They do not drive to Grandma's house or to the home of friends. They drive to the other side of town and meet a needy family—perhaps a struggling single mom or unemployed couple with kids—and shower them with presents and other holiday goodies.

When you develop such a tradition, expect several benefits, the most important of which is making an impression on your children. They learn such truths as people have needs which they can help, that the reason for Christmas is to present gifts of love, as God did in giving His Son. Impression points are all around during such times. When our children are able to see and help the needy and bring them a bit of holiday joy, the focus is no longer merely giving—and getting—family gifts. Both our children and we as parents are reminded that caring for others is an essential part of the Christmas story. The caring acts of an innkeeper, angels (who took time to bring joy to lowly shepherds), and a righteous God can be echoed through acts of holiday compassion.

CHRISTMAS CARD PRAYER

The impression points that can come during the Christmas season can extend to other months of the year. One innovative follow-up to the lessons of Christmas comes from the Gievett family of LaMirada, California. When the Christmas tree comes down, most Christmas greeting cards move to the trash. (A few may join the already overfilled box of past Christmas memories.) The Gievetts arrange their cards neatly into the napkin holder on the dining room table, and a family member retrieves one before each evening meal. The reader scans the card and then the family prays, asking the Lord to bless that particular family or individual.

That's a great way to demonstrate the importance of prayer in the little details of life and to remember those we care for at several times of the year. If you want to avoid the tendency toward "out of sight, out of mind" with those outside your immediate family, add "Christmas Card Prayers" to your meals. You can pull the cards out in January or even the hot days of June (how about both?) to remember the needs of family you care for but don't always see. Who knows, it may even prod your family to make a phone call, or send a letter to those for whom you prayed.

PARENT DATE NIGHT

Every few weeks Ken Mason, otherwise known as Daddy, prepares for his date night. He gets spruced up and heads out to paint the town. But this date is not with Carol, his wife. It is with Josh, his five-year-old son. Joshua and Ken may practice their golf game at the local putt-putt range, or compete for prizes at Joshua's favorite game and pizza spot, Chuck E. Cheese. Whatever activity they plan, these "Dad Date Nights" are the highlight of Joshua's month—and Ken's. It is during such times that Dad and son chat about important topics, or about nothing at all. They just enjoy being together. Ken is earning the right to impress his son's life. Joshua is developing the desire to be like Daddy. As he gets older, the dates with both of his parents (with Dad, training; with Mom, practice) will help him learn how to treat a woman.

Next week, Joshua will have a date with Mommy, while Ken escorts his teenage daughter Becky to dinner and a movie—giving her tips on proper manners, how to act with boys, and why her purity is a priceless gift. Again, an impression is made. For the Mason family, parent-child date nights are a regularly scheduled activity on the calendar—fostering all kinds of wonderfully unscheduled benefits.

FAMILY WORK DAY

At the Davis house every Saturday morning, Mom, Dad, and the kids put on their grubby clothes, eat a hearty breakfast, and head outside for their weekly ritual called Family Work Day. Some would call the routine work: weeds to pull, grass to cut, bushes to trim, a driveway to clean, or trim to paint. But a Family Work Day actually is an excellent way to draw a family together and for parents to work on developing a heritage. Working side by side with family members helps instill an appreciation for the benefits and value of hard work, of course. But there are also experiences that only your family will share; that includes mistakes, laughs, and maybe an occasional sore muscle or blister. Washing windows makes for a better view of the outside but also a time to splash one another (by accident or otherwise) and have a good time together.

When you have a Family Work Day, be sure to make it fun. Dad can provide an added dividend after the last rake is hung and the family has cleaned up; he takes the entire clan out for something enjoyable to reward their united effort. Pizza and a movie, bowling, miniature golf, cream puffs at the local bakery, whatever. Or Mom can pull out her fresh-made lemonade or the carton of Neapolitan ice cream for some do-it-yourself banana splits.

CELEBRATION OF SEXUAL DIFFERENCES

One of the most effective ways to reinforce a child's sexual identity is to celebrate sexual differences. In order to do so, Mom and Dad Ledbetter would capitalize on critical events in the lives of their kids. Dinner and shopping with Mom to celebrate Rebecca's first bra. A weekend trip to celebrate her Becoming a Woman Day—otherwise known as first menstruation. It could be your daughter's first big job, such as baby-sitting a neighbor's child. For boys, other events serve as great opportunities to reinforce sexual identity—such as that first hit in a baseball game or first job (whether mowing lawns or having a paper route.) Maybe your son borrows your razor and shaves his stubble for the first time, or his voice seems to "crack" for several months, changing pitch, and then finally deepening. Maybe he reaches six feet in height, taller than he (or you) expected, or he's a half-inch taller than you. Any of these events are reasons for a Becoming a Man Day.

Recognizing such events has a simple goal: to help your child celebrate those aspects of being male or female that can help set the right angle as it relates to sexual identity. Notice from the suggestions above that his or her sexual identity doesn't depend exclusively on physical changes taking place. The first date or the first job represent for many teenage boys and girls key transition points in the move toward becoming a man or woman. Celebrate them with special outings, cards, or small, meaningful gifts.

CELEBRATION!

As you think of celebrating your child's sexual identity, don't stop there. The best tool for affirmation is celebration, so celebrate everything. It can begin with a toddler saying his first clear sentence, or the first one that makes you smile. As your child has other milestones—it can be his first report card, first baseball victory (or near victory), first teenager paycheck, that first school choir concert—celebrate. Go get ice cream, make a cake, or just buy a congratulations card.

The specifics are not nearly as important as the objective —to celebrate big and small events in the lives of your children. They will feel affirmed. Keep in mind too that the event does not have to be a great success; you are affirming them because of who they are, not what they have accomplished. If they are giving their best efforts, congratulate them for straight C's as much as straight A's, honor them for a great baseball game, even if they lost by a run.

MOM & DAD "MUSH OUT"

The kids are content. The house is calm. Nothing can disturb this serene setting. Until . . . Dad sneaks up behind Mom, wraps his arms around her waist and begins blowing in her ear, whispering sweet nothings, and kissing her neck. Before anyone has a chance to stop them, they are embroiled in a full-blown "mush out." The kids react in horror—"Mom and Dad are up to it again."

"You guys are gross!"

"Yuk!"

"Not again!"

Translation: It's wonderful knowing Mom and Dad love one another.

Nothing creates an environment of love more effectively than a mom and dad "Mush Out." If you're lucky, the kids may just join in by giving you a big bear hug or playfully trying to squeeze your waist. Sometimes, they will "accidentally" wrestle a parent to the floor and a friendly tousle ensues. Such "mushing" can keep families young and loving—and keep children feeling very secure.

WRESTLE MANIA

Wrestling, intentional or otherwise, can be very healthy. Physical touch, so important in communicating love, also benefits several of the five family fragrances: affection, merriment, and affirmation. Larry and Jaylene Cochrun love to tumble with the children when the family is gathered around the television set. The moment a commercial break occurs, all mayhem breaks loose on the den floor. Tackling, wrestling, tickling, headlocks, belly flops, you name it . . . it happens. The end of the commercial signals the end of the round. The children get really sneaky as they try to gain an advantage on Dad by moving into a strategic position during the movie.

In Wrestle Mania, the goals are to get warm, close, laughing, and tired. How you initiate or referee the matches is your choice; the important thing is to do it with gusto and make it fun. At the Cochrun household, a video movie sometimes is interrupted when someone pushes the pause button to declare a round. Almost always, it's Mom who has the remote. Just the push of a button prompts all sorts of family affection and fun.

FAMILY MEMOIRS

"Do you remember when we . . ."

"Yeah, don't we have a picture of us doing that?"

That's all the clue Mom and Dad Trisler needed to break out the family photo albums, the old 8-millimeter home movies, or the videocassettes that hold in trust valuable family memories. Early evening turns into late night as the family tells and retells forgotten events. It actually winds up being a night that the children get a better and more firm grip on just how lucky their family is to have such a bond. "It's surprising how the small differences and arguments we kids had would wither into insignificance after such reminiscing," remembers their oldest daughter, Sherry. Why not grab the old family picture album and spend an evening reliving the ties that bind?

Remember, the above ideas are given in hopes of priming your own creative pump. After a while, you will be able to come up with some of your own. Or maybe you already have. We'd love to know about any ideas that have worked well in your home, too. Contact the Heritage Builders Association (see page 250) and become a member. Join with other families like yours seeking to share great heritage-passing ideas with one another.

NOTES

Chapter 1: An Inheritance of Love

1. Many of the names of individuals have been changed throughout the book to protect privacy.

Chapter 2: The Heritage

1. C. S. Lewis, *Mere Christianity* (New York: Macmillan, 1943), 120.
2. Gary Jackson Oliver and H. Norman Wright, *When Anger Hits Home* (Chicago: Moody, 1992), 69, 29.
3. J. Oswald Sanders, *A Spiritual Clinic* (Chicago: Moody, 1958), 91.

Chapter 3: Your Spiritual Legacy

1. William Martin, *A Prophet with Honor* (New York: William Morrow, 1991), 59.
2. Franklin Graham, *Rebel with a Cause* (Nashville: Nelson, 1995), 39, 120.
3. Ibid., 122.
4. Gloria Gaither, *What My Parents Did Right* (Nashville: Star Song Publishing Group, 1991), 79.
5. J. Oswald Sanders, *A Spiritual Clinic* (Chicago: Moody, 1958), 49.
6. A. W. Tozer, *The Root of the Righteous* (Chicago: Moody, 1955), 61.
7. Albert Siegel, as quoted in Charles Swindoll, *Growing Strong in Family Life* (Portland, Oreg.: Multnomah, 1988), 102.

8. Kurt Bruner, *Responsible Living in an Age of Excuses* (Chicago: Moody, 1992), 84.

9. Ibid.

10. Winston Churchill, as quoted by Ronald Reagan in a nationally televised speech in 1964. Reprinted in the *Wall Street Journal*, 27 October 1994, A20.

11. Some of the findings are quite disturbing to even the casual observer. Here are just a few: "Since 1960, there has been a 560 percent increase in violent crime; more than 400 percent increase in illegitimate births; a quadrupling in divorce rates; a tripling of the percentage of children living in single-parent homes; more than a 200 percent increase in the teenage suicide rate; and a drop of almost 80 points in the S.A.T. scores." See William J. Bennett, *The Index of Leading Cultural Indicators*, 1 (March 1993): i.

Chapter 5: Your Social Legacy

1. Dale Carnegie, *How to Win Friends and Influence People* (New York: Pocket, 1981), xiv.

2. Kurt Bruner, *Responsible Living in an Age of Excuses* (Chicago: Moody, 1992), 148–49.

3. Ibid., 149–50.

4. As cited in Ray Stedman, *From Guilt to Glory* (Waco, Tex.: Word, 1978), 131.

Chapter 6: Choosing What You Will Wear

1. The account of her humiliation and Jesus' response is contained in John 8:3–11.

Chapter 7: The Family Fragrance

1. Gary Smalley and John Trent, *The Blessing* (Nashville: Nelson, 1986), 40–41.

2. Jesus earned such respect while still a child, according to Luke 2:52, as He grew in wisdom and favor among the people.

3. Benjamin Spock, "How Not to Bring Up a Bratty Child," *Redbook*, February 1974, 29–31.

4. Linda Eyre and Richard Eyre, *Three Steps to a Strong Family* (New York: Simon & Schuster, 1994), 39–40.

Chapter 9: The Right Angle

1. M. Scott Peck, *The Road Less Traveled* (New York: Simon & Schuster, 1978), 26.

2. George Gilder, *Men and Marriage* (Getna, La.: Pelican, 1986), 5–6.

Notes

Chapter 10: The Bearings of Tradition

1. Erik H. Erickson, *Identity, Youth and Crisis* (New York: Norton, 1968), 15–19.

Chapter 11: Giving What You Didn't Get

1. Booker T. Washington, *Up from Slavery* (Norwood, Miss.: Norwood, 1900), 84.

Appendix: Priming the Pump

1. Send $9.00 for cost of material, shipping, and handling.
2. For ideas on formulating a Purity Covenant or pledge, as well as such a ceremony, we recommend reading Dawson McAllister and Tim Altman, *Preparing Your Teenager for Sexuality* (Irving, Tex.: Shepherd Ministries, 1988), and Josh McDowell and Dick Day, *Why Wait?* (San Bernardino, Calif.: Here's Life, 1987). For ideas to help your children to say no to sex before marriage, see chapter 10, *Sex, Lies and the Truth* (Wheaton, Ill.: Tyndale, 1994).